2
THE FRENCH PARLIAMENT
Politics in the Fifth Republic

THE FRENCH PARLIAMENT

Politics in the Fifth Republic

Philip M. Williams

GREENWOOD PRESS, PUBLISHERS
WESTPORT, CONNECTICUT

Library of Congress Cataloging in Publication Data

Williams, Philip Maynard.
    The French Parliament.

    Reprint of the ed. published by F. A. Praeger, New
York, which was issued as no. 2 of Studies in political
science.
    Bibliography: p.
    Includes index.
    1. France. Assemblée Nationale, 1946-
2. France--Politics and government--1958-
I. Title.
JN2787.W5 1976   328.44'09   75-32655
ISBN 0-8371-8558-0

Originally published in 1968 by Frederick A. Praeger,
Publishers, New York

Reprinted with the permission of Praeger Publishers, Inc.

Reprinted in 1977 by Greenwood Press, Inc.

Library of Congress Catalog Card Number 75-32655

ISBN 0-8371-8558-0

Printed in the United States of America

Author Williams

PREFACE

This book sets out to give a brief description of the French Parliament in the new constitutional and political conditions of the Fifth Republic. A good deal has been written about the abnormal early years of the new regime, while the Algerian war dominated the scene; this work attempts to redress the balance by discussing the years from 1962 to 1967 when the Gaullists enjoyed a secure majority in the National Assembly. Most of it was written before the 1967 election, but important developments in the first weeks of the third Parliament are mentioned in footnotes.

I owe particular thanks to the help and encouragement of my friends and colleagues at Nuffield College, Oxford, and at the Fondation Nationale des Sciences Politiques and elsewhere in Paris; to David Goldey for his help at all stages from the first draft to proofs; to Jean Brotherhood for secretarial patience beyond the call of duty; and to the constructive criticisms of Malcolm Anderson, Pierre Avril, Vernon Bogdanor, Claude Brosse, François Goguel, Martin Harrison, Roger Hugh, Bill Johnson, Joël Le Theule, Guy Lord, Graham Thomas and Gavin Williams. They have saved me from many errors and blemishes; for those that remain, and for judgments with which they no doubt often disagree, the responsibility is entirely mine.

Oxford
May 1967   PHILIP M. WILLIAMS

CONTENTS

LIST OF TABLES

ABBREVIATIONS

CCC	Comité Consultatif Constitutionnel
CCC	Avis et débats du CCC
★JO	Journal Officiel, Débats de l'Assemblée Nationale
★JO (Senat)	Journal Officiel, Débats du Sénat
MRP	Mouvement Républicain Populaire (Christian Democratic party)
NATO	North Atlantic Treaty Organization
OAS	Organisation de l'Armée Secrète (Algerian European terrorists)
ORTF	Office de Radiodiffusion—Télévision Française
PR	Proportional representation
RDP	Revue du Droit Public et de la Science Politique
RFSP	Revue Française de Science Politique
RI	Républicains Indépendants (Conservative Gaullists)
RPF	Rassemblement du Peuple Français (Gaullist party 1947–53)
TVA	Taxe sur la valeur ajoutée
UNR	Union pour la Nouvelle République (Gaullist party 1958–67)

★ The date is that of the debate, not that of publication.

The Old Regime
and the New Remedies

(I) THE OLD REGIME

'The decline of Parliament' is an old story. Announced by Bryce in 1920, it has characterized a century which, as Wheare has shown, has been hard on legislatures. Many explanations have been offered: the mass electorate; the State's intervention in the economy; the growth of bureaucracy; the need for strong and rapid executive decisions in an age of economic and international crisis; the concentration of public attention and loyalty on heads of government through the mass media; the complexity of modern military and economic problems compared to the (supposedly) simple issues of principle—slavery, home rule for Ireland, relations of Church and State—which dominated the politics of the liberal era. While parliaments may function and even flourish from India to Germany, in their old homes they seem weaker than ever before.

Among the major States, only three have a long-established democratic tradition. In these three countries the legislatures play quite different roles. In the United States, Congress and the Presidency are independent of one another: each can hamper the other's activities but not threaten its existence. But whereas in the last century Congress was often the real originator of policy and source of effective leadership, in recent decades the power of the Presidency has grown overwhelmingly. Congress now rarely takes the lead even in the legislative field proper. Its incapacity to initiate action or dominate policy is seen most clearly when, with a weak President in the White House, the United States suffers from a vacuum of leadership. But its *esprit de corps* remains strong and as an obstructive force Congress can still be very effective, especially when the party opposing the President controls one or both houses. In Great Britain the House of Commons is no longer a forum where cabinets, or even major laws, are created or destroyed. Except in very unusual circumstances the electorate chooses the government, and the government, through party discipline, controls the House of Commons. Almost every important bill is brought in by the cabinet and none passes without its tolerance. Parliament can still play an important role in ventilating the grievances of groups and individuals and in persuading ministers, by argument or by arousing public opinion, to modify their proposals in detail. Sometimes it can veto a measure which never sees the light of day at all. But its most conspicuous function is to provide a forum for criticism and debate, and to conduct over five years the real election campaign which reaches a climax when the house is dissolved.

The French Parliament today is much weaker than the Congress of the United States and somewhat weaker than the British House of Commons. But under the Third and Fourth Republics it was far stronger than either. In contrast to the United States, the French government was responsible to the legislature: in contrast to Britain, the French legislature remained so predominant that for nearly eighty years no ministry dared dissolve. British cabinets were formed by the leaders of the majority party and its discipline gave them power over their nominal parliamentary masters; but in France, government and Parliament alike were paralysed by the number of small parties, the individualism of their members, and the fragility of their coalitions. Moreover, unlike Britain or the United States, France had emerged only recently from authoritarian rule and there were always strong political forces on the far Right or Left (usually both at once) which wanted to scrap the democratic system and revert to autocracy. The threat was the graver because a nineteenth-century French government presided over a powerful and centralized administrative machine, which could be matched neither in the United States with its federal system nor in Great Britain with its flourishing local authorities. The republicans who came to power in the 1870s feared to see this machine controlled either by the authoritarian Right, sheltering behind its royal, imperial or military figureheads, or by the urban revolutionary Left which had been savagely repressed in two bitter civil wars within twenty-five years.

Governments were therefore feared and suspected as natural enemies of liberty who would always abuse the power they wielded. It was the duty, and soon became the pleasure, of self-respecting democrats to keep them firmly in their subordinate place. This attitude was the easier to maintain because the social groups which predominated in the Chamber of Deputies and monopolized the Senate had no desire for governmental action and no expectation of benefits from it (except through protection for home-produced goods). The industrial revolution had never fully come to France, and her farmers, small businessmen and minor provincial notables were content with a regime in which the State conducted foreign policy, organized national defence, kept order at home and defended the currency: Sir John Clapham was to observe that in 1914 France had less 'practical socialism' than any other great industrial country. The local notables did not want any.

Distrusting the capital—the aristocrats of its salons no less than the workers of its suburban factories—they prided themselves on representing the solid provincial backbone of the nation, and watched jealously for signs that their own successful spokesmen were succumbing to the embrace of the powerful and the rich. Ministers were expected to show them a modest deference, and any leader who tried to press them too hard, or to use to the full the powers the constitution allowed him, was likely to incur their permanent displeasure and to be kept from office thereafter by a general conspiracy against him. Strong men therefore found their rare and fleeting opportunities only in a major emergency when a desperate need for immediate leadership and authority overcame the traditional fears and jealousies of the parliamentarians. When crisis struck in the international or perhaps the economic field, and the normal weak and unstable coalition ministries were patently unable to cope with it, Parliament would temporarily waive its cherished sovereignty and allow the government to legislate in its place, or would even abandon all power for a time to a national saviour—preferably a very old man who would show no dangerous ambition once he had served his turn. The emergency over, the hero was quickly pushed back into the limbo from which he should never have emerged. After 1914, the increasing frequency of these grave crises showed that the system was ill-adapted to the new century.

The second world war transformed the balance of power in France, and the political and social groups which had dominated and profited from the Third Republic were discredited by the collapse of 1940 and by their timidity under the German occupation. The new coalition which now came to power embraced hitherto excluded groups: Communist and Socialist workers; nationalist officers and executives who had followed General de Gaulle; Christian Democrats of the new *Mouvement Républicain Populaire* (MRP) who had shown in the Resistance that Roman Catholics could be good republicans. They shared a common objective, the overthrow of the old political system—and a common responsibility for its rapid revival. For their unnatural alliance did not outlast the national crisis which had brought it about, and once France was free their mutual suspicions soon came to prevail. General de Gaulle insisted that the new constitution must establish strong executive leadership independent of Parliament—but in the French political tradition that spelt Bonapartism. All the parties concurred in rejecting his diagnosis, and in believing that the obstacles to action in the old regime came from Parliament's weakness, not its strength: from the indiscipline of the old individualist parties and the obstructive power of the Senate. A government responsible to a predominant National Assembly controlled by organized parties would, they thought, provide both political motive power and democratic control. But there agreement ended. MRP, and in the last resort the

Socialists also, favoured checks and balances to prevent the Communist party establishing its ascendancy; for an omnipotent Assembly controlled by a disciplined revolutionary group was also familiar in French history, and it spelt dictatorship and terror. Manoeuvring between the more dynamic forces opposed to them, the moderate parties narrowly won acceptance of their compromise constitution from a lethargic electorate at the referendum of October 1946.

Within six months both Communists and Gaullists were openly, and in a further six months violently, in opposition to the new Republic they had done so much to create. The ruling parties, bearing the brunt of popular resentment at post-war austerity, now had to call in the old political world to redress the balance of the new: the Radical and Conservative traditionalists became increasingly influential within the governing coalition. These groups, which flourished in the economically backward areas, acquired extra political weight at the expense of the dynamic but dangerous enemies of the system when new electoral laws were passed for the upper house in 1948 and the lower in 1951. These changes helped both to give greater stability to the Fourth Republic and to accentuate its resemblance to the Third, with its weak cabinets; frequent ministerial crises; jealous assertions of parliamentary authority tempered by its occasional abandonment at critical moments; revived indiscipline within the parties; excessive influence of small marginal groups in obstructing change; immense problems in mustering a majority to overcome them; and the exploitation of this confused and confusing situation for factional and personal advantage. Yet the resemblance was never complete, for both in managing Parliament and in running the country the new regime showed (until its last days at least) a marked improvement over the old.

Within Parliament, the Fourth Republic found remedies for several of the weaknesses of the past. Sessions were limited by constitutional amendment in 1954 to a maximum of seven months in the year. Business was made more orderly, and obstruction checked, by gradually increasing the powers of the Presidents' Conference, a committee of parliamentary and party leaders who succeeded in eliminating many (though by no means all) old abuses. A new budgetary procedure, instituted by consent in 1956, sharply curtailed the inordinate time taken while preserving and perhaps improving parliamentary control. The Assembly's finance committee, behaving much more responsibly than in the past, enforced new rules restricting the private member's ancient right to propose public expenditure—to such effect that in March 1958 the deputies agreed to abandon the right altogether. When Parliament temporarily surrendered some of its legislative power to the government, it did so—except over Algeria—under far stricter safeguards and with much more satisfactory results than in the inter-war years. Even the vexed problem of the second chamber, which had been too strong and obstructive in the Third Republic and too weak in the Fourth, was settled by a complicated but satisfactory compromise in the constitutional amendment of 1954.[1]

Such technical improvements could not rescue the reputation of a regime which failed to produce results satisfactory to its citizens. Yet at home it had some striking successes. The despised governments of 1947–50 insisted at high political cost on keeping up the level of investment despite the demagogic criticism of several irresponsible oppositions, and so laid the foundations for the French economic miracle: a rapid growth rate bringing prosperity at last to a proletariat which had been worse off than in most developed countries. Abroad, too, the Fourth Republic worked long and successfully for reconciliation with the hereditary enemy across the Rhine, and launched the policy of European economic union—though the European army project was rejected in the National Assembly in 1954 and the Common Market treaty was only ratified, not implemented, before the advent of de Gaulle. In Tunisia and Morocco Fourth Republican governments undertook decolonization just in time, in Black Africa they began it before a crisis broke. With the accession of a new political generation after 1954, the old jibe lost its force: once France had been 'ruled by men of seventy because the men of eighty are dead', but now, long before Kennedy and Wilson, the Fourth Republic began the vogue for youthful political leadership. Yet these genuine successes and improvements were not enough, and when military sedition threatened the parliamentary republic in 1958, there was no popular rally to its defence as there had been in its past crises.

The regime failed because it was incapable of providing a government with authority. Weak and divided ministries continued to pursue an endless war in Indo-China without daring to demand either the sacrifices implied by a negotiated peace or those required for a serious military effort. In Algeria, repeating the same mistakes, they increasingly surrendered authority into the hands of an army which they could not control and which eventually destroyed them. They overstrained a basically healthy and expanding economy by attempting too much at once and refusing painful choices: they feared entry into the Common Market they had themselves promoted, and were reduced to humiliating mendicancy to protect the value of the currency. And the constant cabinet crises, especially numerous and prolonged in the final year, increasingly exasperated the ordinary Frenchman. Their importance was misunderstood, for most ministers usually stayed in office and much the same men continued to pursue much the same policies. But everyone knew the French political system was a laughing-stock abroad, and this knowledge bred feelings of anger and humiliation

[1]For these reforms see P. M. Williams, *Crisis and Compromise* (London 1964), Chs. 16, 18, 19 and 20; and below, pp. 42, 45, 68, 81.

which sapped the old spirit of republican defence. Just when the country's self-confidence was buttressed by growing prosperity at home, her leaders were conducting a steady and not always dignified retreat abroad. The result was an indignant nationalist reaction against the political system which led even those ardent anti-fascists of twenty years before, Jacques Soustelle and Georges Bidault, to 'prefer to mourn the Fourth Republic rather than *Algérie française*'.

When the ordinary citizen blamed the politicians for the humiliation of his country, he did them a grave injustice. Yet the charge, though grossly exaggerated, was not completely false. More honest and more intelligent than their countrymen allowed, the professional politicians were nevertheless bound by strong ties of mutual solidarity. These feelings of respect and sympathy often eased political tensions and moderated dangerous clashes, but they intensified the hostility against any leader who, like Charles de Gaulle or Pierre Mendès-France, chose to stand outside their club. If by mistake or from necessity they once let such a man get to power, they tried to make doubly certain he should never repeat the performance; and this attitude naturally was noted by and influenced the behaviour of lesser men for whom 'the problem was not only to attain or retain the premiership, but to become premier again'.[2]

Indeed the spirit of parliamentary camaraderie sometimes seemed to extend to a shared mistrust of 'the common enemy, the voter'. The French republican tradition stressed the sovereignty of Parliament and the dangers of direct democracy, for plebiscites were remembered as a dangerous Bonapartist device. In the Third Republic, therefore, the referendum was not allowed and in the Fourth, narrowly confined to constitutional amendments, it was hedged round with legal restrictions and political inhibitions. The politicians tried to prevent by-elections, and detested the idea of dissolution. Even after a general election, the government that first took office rarely lasted long, for frequent shifts in the balance of political power, registered through cabinet crises, ensured that after a short life it would be replaced by successors chosen by the deputies subject to the free play of parliamentary manoeuvres and sentiments. In these conditions it was no wonder that the ordinary voter felt he had no share in choosing his rulers and little responsibility for the fate of the regime.

Yet the citizen himself often brought about the faults he freely imputed to his representatives. When he chose to cast a protest vote for an intransigent opposition party, he helped to limit the democratic politicians' freedom of manoeuvre. For governments had to be drawn from those parties which accepted the democratic system and could be relied on not to use office as an opportunity for subverting it. These parties usually commanded only two-thirds of the seats in the National

[2]M. Duverger, *Demain la République* (Paris 1958), p. 46.

Assembly and sometimes a smaller proportion of the voters (the 1951 electoral law was specially designed to augment their parliamentary representation). But these two-thirds covered the whole spectrum of normal political differences in Great Britain, from Frank Cousins to Enoch Powell, and in addition they were divided by an ancient quarrel no longer politically significant across the Channel: the dispute about the relations of Church and State, especially in education. Since even a small defection in the democratic ranks could bring a government down, the voter who helped elect an intransigent supporter or opponent of lower taxes, or drastic social reforms, or aid to church schools, was thereby weakening the governmental coalition and contributing to ministerial instability. Impatiently insisting on the demands of his sectional group, threatening to change his vote if the inevitable compromise left him dissatisfied, he constrained his party to take up rigid positions which might well lead to a government crisis—for which he would blame the politicians. Thus the personal and factional intrigues of the deputies merely aggravated a far more serious situation: it was the lack of a majority in Parliament (because there was none in the country) which made unstable government inevitable. As if this were not enough, France was the only country which had both a great empire and a strong Communist party. Without the Communists the shrivelled democratic Left and progressive Centre could not muster a majority for decolonization; but with Communist support came fears for domestic stability and international tranquillity which alienated Centre votes and in turn made it impossible to find a majority. It was over imperial and not domestic problems that tension and bitterness were worst, and it was Algeria, not the class war, that destroyed the Fourth Republic and menaced French democracy itself.

(II) THE NEW REMEDIES

Swept to power by the crisis in Algiers, the Gaullist makers of the new constitution imposed a complete break with the old republican tradition. The deputies had accepted de Gaulle as prime minister only because he was the one alternative to civil war, and he made it a condition of his acceptance that his government—which included the principal leaders of the Fourth Republican parties—be temporarily granted full powers, including the power to draft a new constitution. The government's draft was submitted to a Constitutional Consultative Committee (CCC) of thirty-nine members, one-third government nominees and two-thirds parliamentarians; although the latter were acutely conscious of their unpopularity in the country they made several efforts to amend the draft in the traditional direction. Most of their main suggestions were ignored, however, except for those concerning the Community into which France's overseas empire was

B

(not for long) transformed. Otherwise the constitution of the Fifth Republic, submitted for the approval of the nation in the referendum of September 28, 1958, was little changed from the government's original proposals.

Michel Debré, who as minister of justice presided over the drafting operations, claimed that the new provisions were intended to restore, or rather establish, a parliamentary system in France.[3] In practice many of them seemed to indicate a determination to keep the legislature in its place. For the constitution-makers (even those of parliamentary outlook and experience like Debré) were clear that Parliament could properly perform only a limited range of functions and must, given the French tradition of legislative sovereignty, be carefully confined within that range if it was not to dissipate its own energies and the government's authority. These limits restricted the members both in the ways they could criticize and supervise the government, and in their handling of legislation and finance.

In the first place the government, though responsible to the parliamentary majority, was no longer to be representative of it or necessarily selected from it. To Gaullists, the country's first need was a strong executive power, capable of making difficult choices speedily and decisively; experience had proved that such a power could never be based on the shifting sands of parliamentary coalitions. The President must therefore be chosen outside Parliament: originally by a large electoral college mainly of local councillors, after 1962 by direct popular vote. He would nominate the premier who would then choose his ministers; any of them who was an MP would have to resign his seat. The principle of governmental responsibility to the Assembly was preserved, since the ministry would need the approval of the deputies who could turn it out subsequently by a motion of censure; the President of the Republic could then dissolve (but only once in a year). A series of elaborate devices ensured that only a determined majority of the whole house could remove the government, which was carefully protected from the guerilla tactics by which oppositions used to harass ministers on minor points until they became vulnerable to a direct assault. While the deputies could still express their criticisms on specific points, they could not press their attacks to a vote. These rigid rules, the fruit of bitter experience in an Assembly with no coherent majority, were to have unexpected effects in the new regime where the first three National Assemblies (especially the second) had majorities loyal to the government. For while the limitations could not save a cabinet if the majority of the house turned against

[3] *La Nouvelle Constitution*, p. 2. This is Debré's speech introducing the constitution before the *Conseil d'Etat* on 27 August 1958. It is reprinted in *Revue francaise de science politique* (hereafter *RFSP*) 9.1, Jan. 1959: for Debré's claim see p. 7.

it, they could and did frustrate a minority which tried to use Parliament as a forum for appealing to public opinion against the policies of the country's rulers. But the critics suffered equally from their own incapacity to adapt to the new situation, in which the majority could no longer be split and the ministry brought down by a judicious attack mounted at the right moment against a weak sector of the government's support. Thus relations between ministers and members were wholly transformed. The deputies had lost the right of choosing a government, though not that of overthrowing it; ministers could not be or remain members of either house, though they could still speak in Parliament;[4] there were opportunities to criticize but they were used inadequately, partly because the rules prevented them being exploited to harass and undermine the government, and partly because few of the critics could conceive of any other way of using them.

In the second place the newly renovated Parliament was, of course, to vote the laws and the budget. But here, too, old practices were prohibited or transformed by the new masters. The government was at last to have the assurance that it could get its business through in reasonable time and more or less in the form it desired (always subject to the Assembly's power to throw it out). The parliamentary timetable, hitherto determined with remarkable inefficiency by the house itself, was now—except for one sitting a week reserved for 'questions'—made subject to the cabinet's discretion. Government legislation would therefore absorb most of Parliament's time. It would still be discussed in committees of the house, but these would be far less dangerous than in the past. They were to be fewer and more broadly based, and they could no longer mutilate a bill before presenting it to their colleagues. In the past the house had discussed the committee's draft of bills, often quite different from that introduced by the government, which then had an uphill struggle to try to restore its own version.[5] Now the minister piloted his bill through the house in the form in which he introduced it, and the committee was obliged to move amendments—and amendments not previously discussed in committee were (in theory) disallowed. Moreover, the minister was well protected against any attack, for he could refuse to allow a separate vote on awkward clauses or amendments, and insist on a 'package vote' on a version of the whole measure in a form acceptable to him. The government could even carry a bill without any vote at all by making it a matter of confidence, in which case it passed unless the opposition could find a clear majority of the entire house to turn the ministry out. For dealing with differences between the two houses,

[4]French ministers (who before 1958 were nearly always MPs) have always been allowed to speak in either house.
[5]The Fourth Republic, unlike the Third, had allowed it to ask the deputies to debate its original draft instead of the committee's. It rarely did.

a new mechanism was invented, which at every stage could be operated only by the government; the ministers thus acquired the possibility either (as was thought likely) of calling in the supposedly solid and reliable Senate as an ally against the turbulent and irresponsible Assembly, or else of using the lower house to overcome unexpected obstruction in the upper. The members' right to propose public expenditure, greatly curtailed during the Fourth Republic, was wholly abolished in the Fifth. The budget, which had taken so long before the reform of 1956, was now subjected to a rigid timetable and might even be enforced by the government on its own authority if Parliament was dilatory.[6]

Still more striking were the new limitations on the sphere of parliamentary action. Preoccupied with trivial matters, Parliament had too often neglected difficult and dangerous problems at home and even more overseas; when these reached a critical stage, it had found itself obliged to hand over its legislative authority for a time to the executive it feared and suspected. In the new constitution, the questions on which Parliament was entitled to legislate were specifically enumerated, and it was excluded altogether from all the rest. The new restrictions, by freeing members from the clutter of trivial details, enabled them to act more effectively on the important questions. But the terms in which the restrictions were defended revealed that the Gaullists regarded Parliament as an essentially obstructive force, and wanted to withdraw from its purview those problems on which they were eager to undertake reforms.[7] Moreover, even where Parliament was normally the master, special powers might still be delegated by it to the government and might now, in a great emergency, be assumed on his own authority by the President of the Republic.

The new constitution, therefore, enshrined the Gaullists' ambivalent attitude to Parliament. On' the one hand, in principle they were democrats who believed that the strong government France required had to be founded on popular acceptance of its legitimacy, and therefore needed the approval of the people and their representatives. On the other, in practice they viewed those representatives with much more suspicion than the people themselves. They thought that the political class of the Third and Fourth Republics had lost sight of the basic interests of the nation; had submerged effective government under the pressures of minority interests, personal rivalries and outdated suspicions; and had exploited the representative system for its own ends—preserving an obviously inadequate political structure solely in order to pursue private quarrels and ambitions in the 'house

[6]Not, of course, if the budget was voted on and rejected within the time-limit.
[7]See the statements of M. Janot, the government's spokesman at the CCC; *Avis et débats du Comité Consultatif Constitutionnel* (Paris 1960: hereafter *CCC*), pp. 104, 106–7.

without windows'. If democracy was interpreted to mean only opposition to the government, it could not long survive in the twentieth
century world; strong measures would therefore be required to root
out so pernicious a tradition.

The need for a real authority was paramount, both to meet the
inevitable external crises and to enforce domestic reforms which Parliament, on past form, would only obstruct. But this executive could not
safely be based on Parliament because the French electorate was so
divided that no coherent majority could be expected to emerge. Britain
could draw its government from a House of Commons with a coherent
and disciplined party majority; but 'because in France governmental
stability cannot result primarily from the electoral law, it must result
from making constitutional rules, and that is what gives this proposal
its decisive explanation and its historical justification'.[8] Once the new
executive authority was securely established, Parliament could within
limits play a useful role. But the limits must be enforced with the
utmost rigour to prevent the members using their remaining powers
to reclaim those they had enjoyed, and were now to lose. Nor could
the representative system remain the exclusive channel for the popular
will to express itself. The executive must be allowed to appeal from
Parliament to the electorate, either by dissolving the Assembly or by
submitting to referendum the most important bills, especially on
constitutional matters. Hitherto the parliamentarians had both denied
the necessary power of the executive and misused the authority they
drew from the people, who had grown disillusioned with politics and
disaffected from the State. To the Gaullists, the Fifth Republic would
be far more democratic than its predecessors.[9]

Under the new regime the Parliament of France, once among the
most powerful in the world, became one of the weakest. Even its own
standing orders had to be submitted for approval to a new Constitutional Council.[10] Its legislative powers and its opportunities to vote
against the government were limited. Though ministers were responsible to it as in Britain, they were not members of it and they had more
control than British ministers over its proceedings. Above all the real
source of policy was the President of the Republic, neither chosen
by Parliament nor responsible to it, who could dissolve it or (in practice

[8]Debré, loc. cit., p. II (and in RFSP, loc. cit., p. 17). On assumptions about
the electoral law see below, pp. 23–4, 26–8, 102.

[9]As René Capitant has argued cogently and consistently, notably in his
articles in Notre République nos. 60–63 (20 Sept., 4 and 18 Oct., 1 Nov. 1962)
and in Les Institutions politiques de la France (debate sponsored by the Association française de science politique, February 1964), pp. 21–25.

[10]Comprising three nominees each of the Presidents of the Republic, Assembly
and Senate; and ex-Presidents of the Republic. Among its other duties it also
settled disputed elections (formerly decided, often badly, by the house concerned).

if not in theory) by-pass it by a direct appeal to the people at a referendum. Until 1958 the French legislature had clung to more power than its British or American counterparts, but had used that power negatively and ineffectively. Now it found itself weaker than either.

II

New Men
in Power

(1) ELECTIONS AND ASSEMBLIES, 1958–67

At the referendum of September 1958 the new constitution was over-whelmingly approved by the people. Every important party but the Communists had prudently endorsed it, and at the November election the politicians competed in their professed devotion to de Gaulle and his programme. The voters, however, had observed the hesitations and divisions of the left-wing parties during the May crisis, and in their determination to give de Gaulle the popular mandate he sought, they naturally assumed he would best be helped by those who had worked hardest and longest to bring him to power.

Even the new electoral system conspired to the advantage of the political forces it had been intended to check. While the other new rules were at least supposed to be permanent, the electoral law was regarded in the bad old French tradition as a temporary measure adopted for reasons of momentary political convenience. Under the Third Republic most general elections were fought under *scrutin d'arrondissement*: single-member constituencies with majority voting in which, if no candidate had a clear majority of the votes cast, a second ballot was held at which the man with most votes won.[1] This system allowed neighbouring parties to compete fiercely at the first ballot but combine at the second; it had helped well-known local figures and parties of the centre. Discredited in 1945, it was replaced by propor-tional representation (PR), which then enjoyed overwhelming support. But PR soon lost favour, and in 1951, with both Communists and Gaullists in violent opposition to the regime, the Fourth Republican parties amended the electoral law to benefit those political groups—namely themselves—which were capable of making alliances against their various intransigent opponents.

In 1958 the Gaullists were determined to substitute a new electoral system for one which no one now defended. Many of their leaders, especially Jacques Soustelle, favoured a close alliance with Conserva-

[1] To win at the first ballot it was also necessary to poll at least a quarter of the registered electorate.

tive and other party chieftains who wanted to win the Algerian war at
any cost. But de Gaulle, preferring a divided National Assembly to one
which might tie his hands, decided in favour of the Left—Pierre
Mendès-France as well as Guy Mollet—who were now advocating a
return to the pre-war arrangements. The new law differed in minor
ways from the old system: candidates with under 5 per cent of the
first-ballot vote could not stand at the second, held one week later.[2]
Seats were redistributed, with an average of 93,000 inhabitants for
each constituency; very small departments (which are usually poor
and rural, and often left-wing) were over-represented; most big towns
were split up, to the disadvantage of the Communist party; but on
the whole the allocation was reasonably fair. It was hoped that this
electoral change would prevent too complete a victory for the most
vociferous champions of General de Gaulle—and of an intransigent
policy in Algeria which, though this as yet was not clear, was far from
being his. On past experience the new law should have helped moderate men against extremists and established politicians against newcomers: Communists and the far Right would thus be hampered, and
de Gaulle's allies among the Fourth Republican parties somewhat
protected against the onslaught of his turbulent and potentially
embarrassing UNR supporters.

These expectations, reasonable in themselves, were shared by the
prospective victims and beneficiaries alike, and by neutral observers
as well. But they proved erroneous. The Communists were indeed the
main sufferers under the new system—as a result of the abolition of
PR, the loss of a third of their votes, and the disciplined determination
with which all other Frenchmen used the second ballot to defeat
them. Sitting members, too, were unpopular: only 28 per cent of the
deputies standing for re-election were returned. The Socialists and the
Radicals did badly; MRP held their own better than they had expected;
the Conservatives gained seats but did not win the triumph they had
counted on. The real victors were the new Gaullist party, the Union
for the New Republic (UNR), which did well at the first ballot and
spectacularly at the second.[3] It was not the Socialists, as had been
expected, but the UNR who profited from the central position, pick-
ing up anti-Communist votes in left-wing districts and anti-Conserva-
tive votes in right-wing areas. They emerged with 188 seats in France,
and over 200 in all, more than any French party (save the Radicals in
1910) had ever won.

[2]The law applied to few overseas constituencies; for the varying rules in force
there see P. M. Williams & M. Harrison, *De Gaulle's Republic* (London 1960),
pp. 252–3. In 1966 these rules were slightly altered. For the 1967 election the
Paris area had five extra seats, and candidates could contest the second ballot
only if they had polled over 10% of the registered electorate at the first.

[3]Although 39 seats were filled on the first round, the UNR polled 1,200,000
more votes on the second.

Yet the election was fought on false premises. The parties which
won were those that seemed the most devoted to General de Gaulle;
they were also those whose leading spokesmen most loudly proclaimed
their determination to keep Algeria French. Some of their members
took a long time to realize that they owed their success to the first
factor rather than the second. As the General's Algerian policy shifted
more and more in a liberal direction, a growing strain was put on the
consciences—or electoral calculations—of these deputies; conversely,
left-wingers, however critical over foreign or domestic policy, became
more favourable to the government on the problem that overshadowed
all the rest. The politics of the first Parliament were determined by
this evolution. At first the UNR and the old-style Conservatives—also
represented in the government—were rivals for power rather than
opponents over policy.[4] Most of their parliamentary leaders were so
vociferously for *Algérie française* that left-wing opinion encouraged
the President to ignore the Assembly, fearing that an assertion of its
power would impede any progress with the problem. But in September
1959 de Gaulle announced that Algeria was to have self-determination,
and in subsequent months his various critics—in Parliament, among
the Algerian settlers and in the army—failed in their challenges to the
new policy. Dismissed in February 1960, Jacques Soustelle became
the leader of a new Algerian opposition, which won over many
Conservatives, a few from the other Fourth Republican parties,
most European (though few Moslem) deputies from Algeria, and a tiny
fraction of the UNR. For the rest of this Parliament, therefore, the
government faced a right-wing opposition which was much stronger
in the Assembly than in the country, and a left-wing opposition which
was under-represented among the deputies. But the former would not
support left-wing domestic measures and the latter would not oppose
the President on Algeria, so that with the loyal support of the largest
party in the house, the government was not in danger.

Nevertheless, in two areas its opponents could come together. First,
all the Fourth Republican parties resented the way Parliament was
humiliated by a President who soon abandoned his lofty status above
the political battle to become the effective maker of policy. Their
irritation found particularly vigorous expression in the Senate.
Secondly, they all defended the Atlantic alliance and European unity,
and deplored de Gaulle's departures from them; this was the main
reason for the dismissal in January 1960 of Antoine Pinay, which
shook the Conservatives' fragile loyalty to the government. Soustelle
and many other *Algérie française* leaders had been strongly nationalist
and anti-American in the past, but now they were eager to find allies

[4]The Socialists left office over economic policy at the end of 1958, and MRP
over European policy in May 1962; some Conservatives have held office
throughout.

against the President. However, the Left and Centre opposition was unwilling to defeat the government and risk a dissolution of Parliament —for fear both of electoral disaster, and of giving a dangerous opportunity to the right-wing enemies of democracy in the army and elsewhere. Consequently the conflicts over foreign policy, though a serious cause of dissatisfaction among the politicians, were never pressed to an extreme during the Algerian war.

Peace was made in March 1962, and the political crisis followed within six months. The parties had convinced themselves that Gaullism was a passing nightmare, and that once the General had served his turn by settling the war, they could dispense with him and revert to 'politics as usual'. De Gaulle first made a half-hearted effort to conciliate them, replacing Michel Debré, prime minister since 1959, by Georges Pompidou. But whereas Debré was an old parliamentarian, Pompidou was merely an old confidant of the President's who had never been elected to anything. His appointment therefore aroused some parliamentary resentment, which he tried to appease by offering posts to Edgar Faure, a talented Radical conciliator from the Fourth Republic, and Pierre Pflimlin, the respected leader of MRP. But Faure refused and then de Gaulle, by an intransigent statement on European policy, provoked all the MRP ministers to resign. The old parties now confidently expected to regain at the next general election, due in the spring of 1963, all the support they had lost at the previous one. But the General outmanoeuvred them. After a narrow escape from assassination in August, he announced a bill for direct election of future Presidents of the Republic by popular vote. He proposed, unconstitutinally, to submit the bill to referendum without first sending it to Parliament, where the Senate would certainly reject it. As he probably intended, this procedure provoked the National Assembly at its October meeting to censure the government (by a majority of forty); he promptly dissolved it, and won a striking and unexpected victory at the election in November.

This time it was the Right, now in opposition after profiting from its professed Gaullism in 1958, which suffered the worst defeat; half its votes and three-quarters of its seats were lost, and apologists for the OAS (the terrorist defenders of *Algérie française*) were eliminated from the Assembly. The other Fourth Republican parties also lost votes, especially MRP. The Communists failed to regain any;[5] but this time the Socialists and Radicals were willing to contract second-ballot alliances with them and so the Left, while losing votes, emerged with sixty more seats in the new house. Once again, however, the real victory went to the UNR, whose spectacular increase in votes came this time on the first ballot rather than the second: a sign they were

[5]Except perhaps at the second ballot: see my article in *Parliamentary Affairs*, 16.2 (Spring 1963), p. 171.

winning support in their own right, not just as a lesser evil than their rivals. With 233 deputies they were only eight short of a clear majority in the Assembly. The necessary votes were comfortably made up by the thirty Republican Independents, Conservative Gaullists who in the referendum or afterwards broke with their party to support the President. Should they ever defect there were volunteers on other benches (notably MRP's) who would willingly replace them. In the second Parliament, therefore, the government could dispose of a majority far more homogeneous and secure than in the first.

After the general election Pompidou slightly reconstructed his ministry, which remained in office almost without change for three years, reinforcing the impression of stable government which was such an asset to the Gaullists in the country. With the war over, the ministers could now concentrate their energies on domestic affairs. They still had difficulties with the Senate, but the majority in the Assembly— no longer strained by the passions of the war, and grateful to the President whose popularity had won them their seats—remained steadfastly loyal. Under the new constitution the government and the deputies together could always override the upper house, which could win no legislative battles, feared to provoke its own abolition, and therefore did not systematically obstruct. The second Parliament was thus able to pass an impressive legislative programme. By the autumn of 1965 the old parties were in disarray, patently unable to present a coherent alternative government, and opinion polls were showing that the ministry as well as the President enjoyed unusual popularity. The Gaullists therefore faced the presidential election without qualms, and it was a severe shock when the General won only 44 per cent of the vote on the first ballot (and only 55 per cent on the second).[6] During the fifteen months that preceded the next general election, Gaullist and opposition parties alike concentrated on the battle to control the next National Assembly with an intensity which certainly did not suggest that Parliament had no importance under the new regime.

The Gaullists tried to regain the lost ground by a reshuffle of the cabinet and a modification of its policies. The modernizing programme and abrasive personality of Edgard Pisani, minister of agriculture, was blamed for peasant defections at the presidential election; he was promoted and replaced by Edgar Faure. Michel Debré came back as minister of finance, succeeding the Republican Independents' leader Valéry Giscard d'Estaing, but he found that the economic situation gave little scope for the expansionist policies he favoured. Different

[6]He seems to have offended the electorate by taking his victory for granted and by ignoring the succession problem; the result probably represented not a loss of support for Gaullism, but the defection of many who had previously voted for the General but not for the UNR. See my article in *ibid.*, 19.1 (Winter 1965–6), pp. 19, 29–30.

viewpoints within the majority were actively encouraged for a time, and while Giscard celebrated his new freedom by asserting the independence of the Gaullist Conservatives, Pisani, Faure and other ministers showed sympathy with the small but articulate minority of Left Gaullists. But the prime minister soon called a halt to this fragmentation and successfully insisted that the majority must fight the coming election with only one 'Fifth Republic' candidate in each seat. Giscard's followers won a few concessions, and some twenty deputies from other parties were given the official coupon, but the great majority of Gaullist candidates naturally came from the UNR. The opposition parties were thus obliged to strengthen their own discipline. The alliance of the Left, belatedly patched together on a local basis at the 1962 election, was this time nation-wide and clear-cut. Consequently the Right and Centre opponents of Gaullism could no longer make local deals with the non-Communist Left, and found themselves squeezed between two stronger rivals like British Liberals. Unable to establish their credibility as an alternative government, they were forced to seek—in vain—for concessions from the majority.

The election of March 1967 was the first since the war to occur at the normal legal date, the first for a generation to take place when no crisis threatened France, and the first in her history to pass judgment on a government which had held office throughout the expiring Parliament. More clearly than ever before the electorate chose stability. The Gaullists gained two million votes, mainly in the rural south, while the conservative opposition sank even below the disaster level of 1962. But the Left also profited from its new-found cohesion, especially in the industrial areas. At the first ballot the Communists gained a million votes and their allies half a million; at the second their combined strength, reinforced by unexpectedly numerous anti-Gaullists of the Right and Centre, brought the Left forty extra seats and allowed the 'Democratic Union for the Fifth Republic' only a wafer-thin majority—to which Giscard's increased following was now indispensable. The electorate had shown both its satisfaction with the regime, and its dissatisfaction with the policies and style of the government.[7]

(II) THE NEW SENATE

In 1958 Michel Debré had expected 'an Assembly too aggressive because it is too divided' and, to meet this danger, had tried to

[7] Any expectation that the warning would be heeded was instantly shattered by the government's demand for special legislative powers over economic and social matters (below, p. 54). The voters had returned a much more critical Parliament and the constitution was at once invoked to reduce it to impotence. On the election see P. M. Williams and D. B. Goldey in *Parliamentary Affairs* 20.3 (Summer 1967).

TABLE I

Elections and Parliaments in the Fifth Republic

	Gaull[1]	Cons[2] etc.	MRP[2]	Rad[3][4] etc.	Soc[4]	Comm	Non-Voters	Total[5]
1. Votes (millions: France only)								
1956	0·8	3·1	2·4	3·2	3·2	5·5	4·6	26·8
1958 (i)	4·2	4·5	2·4	1·8	3·2	3·9	6·2	27·2
1962 (i)	6·6	1·7	1·6	1·8	2·3	4·0	8·6	27·5
1967 (i)	8·5	— 2·9 —		— 4·7 —		5·0	5·4	28·3
1958 (ii)	5·2	3·9	1·7	1·1	2·5	3·7	6·1	
1962 (ii)	6·4	1·2	0·8	1·2	2·3	3·2	6·1	
1967 (ii)	8·0	— 1·3 —		— 4·7 —		4·0	5·0	
2. % of electorate								
1956	3	12	9	12	12	21	17	
1958 (i)	15	17	9	7	12	14	23	
1962 (i)	24	6	6	7	8	15	31	
1967 (i)	30	— 10 —		— 17 —		18	19	
3. National Assembly (incl. overseas)								(seats)[6]
1956	22	97	84	94	99	150		596
1958	206	129	56	40	47	10		552
1962	268	— 55 —		43	66	41		482
1967	242	— 41 —		— 121 —		73		487
4. Senate (incl. overseas)								
1958 (Apr.)	39	90	26	65	56	16		319
1959	44	94	34	64	51	14		307
1965	30	79	38	49	52	14		274

[1]Incls. RI 1962 and 1967.

[2]In C. Dem. 1967; excls. Extr. Right (0·5m. 1958, 0·2m. 1962 and 1967) and Miscellaneous (1·1 and 0·7m., largely Cons.) in 1967.

[3]Incls. right-wing Rads. 1956 (under 1m.), miscellaneous Left later (about 0·4m. 1958 and 1962).

[4]In Fed. of the Left 1967.   [5]About 1m. persons of voting age do not register.

[6]Main groups not shown: in the Assembly, Poujadists (2·6m. and 52 seats in 1956) and Algerian integrationists (66 in 1958); in the Senate, Overseas Independents (23 in 1958).

strengthen 'a Senate whose principal role is to support the government in case of need' against the deputies.[8] He tried to identify the upper house with the new regime by lengthening its members' term, adapting its electoral college to choose the President of the Republic also, giving its President higher formal precedence and making him acting President of the Republic in case of a vacancy. Indeed one Gaullist constitutional expert—and future senator—was rash enough to prophesy that President, premier and Senate would together form 'a single bloc ... mainstay and motive force of'the Fifth Republic'.[9] But

[8]*Loc. cit.*, pp. 10–11 (and *RFSP* 9.1, Jan. 1959, p. 17).

[9]M. Prélot, *Pour comprendre la nouvelle constitution* (Paris 1959), p. 54.

here again the expectations of the constitution-makers were to be falsified.

Elections for the upper house are almost impervious to national moods and swings, for the Senate cannot be dissolved, and only a third of its members are elected at a time.[10] These contests need not occur at moments of political tension, and even when they do—as in 1962, just before the constitutional referendum, and in 1965, before the presidential election campaign—they have aroused no interest and led to no changes: a striking sign of the low political status of the upper house.[11] Except in 1946–48, senators have always been chosen in each department by an electoral college consisting mainly of local councillors. The distribution of seats among departments strengthens the countryside against the towns; and within each electoral college the large towns are seriously under-represented (though slightly less than in the Fourth and much less than in the Third Republic). Moreover, since most senators need a clear majority of votes cast for election on the first ballot, and an ordinary majority on the second, the minority of urban electors can rarely win a seat. But proportional representation is used in the seven most populous departments (which return five or more senators each and sixty in all); this helps the rural minorities in urban areas—but also ensures that the Communists and Gaullists win seats in their strongholds and so obtain some, though inadequate, representation in the upper house. For all these reasons its electoral system makes the Senate a bastion of 'backward France', dominated by regions, occupations and attitudes which are steadily losing political weight. The rural, propertied outlook of its members was vividly displayed on an amnesty bill in 1966. In generous (or opposition-minded) mood they extended the measure sent up to them by the deputies to embrace many more offences: electoral fraud, inciting disaffection in the army, insulting the President, libelling ministers and foreign dignitaries. They excluded only one misdemeanour: poaching.[12]

Rural or urban, the electoral colleges in each department consist of local politicians, predisposed towards men well known for their activity in local government, where a successful mayor can make a reputation and win support extending far beyond the ranks of his own party. Here was another handicap for the Gaullists. In March 1959, when all the country's municipal councils came up for their periodical re-election, the crisis atmosphere of the previous year had already passed and the government was unpopular because of its recent austerity

[10]See below, p. 36.

[11]J. Chapsal, *La vie politique en France depuis* 1940 (Paris 1966), pp. 467, 547 (on 1962 only).

[12]*JO* (*Sénat*), 24 May 1966, pp. 611–8. On rural over-representation see E. Guichard-Ayoub *et al.*, *Etudes sur le Parlement de la Ve République* (Paris 1965), pp. 1–41.

programme. The Gaullist assault on the town halls was easily beaten off, and the senatorial election which followed in April completed 'the revenge of the Fourth Republic'. At this election, exceptionally, the entire Senate was being chosen together to inaugurate the new constitutional regime. Of the former members who stood again, 84 per cent held their seats—as only 28 per cent of the deputies had done in the previous November. The newcomers included two dozen former deputies returning triumphantly to Parliament after a few months out, among them men of experience and authority such as Gaston Defferre, François Mitterrand, Jean Lecanuet and Edgar Faure; at once, therefore, the Senate became a forum for the vigorous and critical debate which at that time was not much encouraged in an impatient and intolerant Assembly.

Peopled by notables of the traditional kind, who were sent there by the very intermediaries that the Gaullists despise and denounce, the Luxembourg Palace soon stood out as the opposition fortress within the regime. It was clearly dominated by old republicans of conservative outlook (notably its Radical and Socialist members); the government's administrative reforms were quite as unpopular there as its cavalier treatment of Parliament.[13] At first the conflict merely reflected an incompatibility of temper between the elders of the defunct regime and the masters of the new one. But it turned into a bitter personal feud when in 1962 Gaston Monnerville, the Senate's perennial President, denounced in unmeasured terms the unconstitutional procedure by which de Gaulle was introducing direct election to the Presidency.[14] In the next few years ministers were normally forbidden to speak in the Senate (not one did so during 1965) and it was permitted to deal only with lowly ministers of state (*secrétaires d'Etat*). The President of the Republic no longer extended official hospitality to the President of the Senate or shook his hand at formal functions. There were frequent public and private proposals (or threats) to reform the Senate by amalgamating it with the Economic and Social Council, a slightly shadowy body of pressure-group representatives and official nominees which produced many well-digested reports on social and economic problems and enjoyed some discreet influence behind the scenes.[15]

These suggestions did the Gaullists no political harm, since the

[13]For examples of the conservatism of the Socialist senators see *JO* (*Sénat*), 23 June 1966, pp. 970–2 (in defence of the economic privileges of barristers); 9 Nov. 1966, especially pp. 1442–5, 1471 (on local government reform).

[14]Speaking at a Radical party conference, he condemned the prime minister, who was technically responsible, for *forfaiture* (criminal dereliction of duty).

[15]For the Council's composition see Williams and Harrison, pp. 254–5; and for its working, J. E. S. Hayward, *Private Interest and Public Policy* (London 1966).

Council gave the younger leaders of industry, agriculture and the trade unions better representation than the Senate itself. The idea of bringing these 'new notables' to sit beside the old therefore won approval from the most progressive leaders of the pressure-groups; indeed, it had been put forward earlier by modernizers in the opposition such as Pierre Mendès-France.[16] It was the old parties which vigorously opposed it, the Communists particularly distinguishing themselves as defenders of the 'Republican Senate'. But Gaullist enthusiasm for the reform diminished when the Economic Council itself showed signs of rebelliousness over the Fifth Plan, and when the presidential election of December 1965 cast doubt on de Gaulle's ability to carry a new referendum proposal. The government was in no hurry, for in politics as in chess the threat may be stronger than the execution: hope of postponing and fear of provoking the evil day helped to moderate the vigour of senatorial opposition. Meanwhile the old notables were the target of the Gaullists, who had strengthened them in 1958, and the favourites of the old Left, which had then condemned the constitution for entrenching the forces of conservatism in the upper house. Once again the opposition appeared as spokesmen of the past.

(III) THE MEMBERSHIP

In social as well as political composition the Senate represented the country's traditional political personnel, while the Assembly was much more open to the winds of change. There are even fewer senators from among the poor (workers, clerks, elementary schoolteachers) than in the Fourth Republic—though still more than there were before the war. Otherwise the Fifth Republic continues trends already apparent in the Fourth: more businessmen and many more farmers, both increasing at the expense of the professions; and an average age which fell sharply just after the war (from sixty-one to fifty) but has since then climbed steadily back as members grew old in their seats.[17]

In the less stable National Assembly the picture was less clear-cut. There the upheaval of 1958 reduced the number of working-class deputies to seven, the fewest since 1885, and those from poor backgrounds from 21 per cent over the whole Fourth Republic to 7 per

[16]*Ibid.*, Ch.V. on attitudes to the reform proposals.

[17]To 55 by 1959 and 60 by 1965. For senators see L. Hamon, 'Members of the French Parliament', *International Social Science Journal* 13.4 (1961), pp. 552–3; for deputies, M. Dogan in Association française de Science politique, *Le Référéndum. . . et les élections de. . . 1958*, Paris 1960, pp. 241–78, and in *ibid. . . . 1962*, Paris 1965, pp. 429–32. Table II is based on an adaptation of their figures, except for 1936 (from anon., *A Constitution for the Fourth Republic*, Washington, D.C., 1947, p. 82).

cent: [18] they regained some of the lost ground in 1962, and a little more in 1967.

Agriculture dropped slightly at each election, while business rose sharply in 1958, from 16 to 23 per cent, and by another 1 per cent in 1962. The professions, dominant as always, provided just half the total of deputies in 1962—a little more than in the Fourth Republic but far below the 57 per cent of 1958. They dropped back slightly, and business abruptly, with the Left's gains in the third Parliament. These changes tended to reflect party fortunes, for most working-class deputies are Communists, most teachers are Socialists, and a high proportion of parliamentary farmers are Conservatives.[19] Two-thirds of the UNR and Conservative members elected in 1958 had been to university (among British Conservative MPs in 1959, only 60 per cent had). Their members were likelier than those of the other parties to have a technical, mathematical or military training instead of the traditional law and letters. Medicine (a profession which produces many politicians in France) enjoyed a new boom with the return to single-member seats, but law recovered no ground in 1958 and lost even more in 1962 and 1967.[20]

While the outgoing deputies were slaughtered in unprecedented numbers, the new men were not altogether new: except for thirty-three in 1958 and fifty-seven in 1962 (each time all UNR but six), all had had political experience in the Fourth Republic, almost always as parliamentary candidates or as local councillors. The age-level dropped sharply in 1958, with deputies under forty outnumbering those over fifty (in 1936 and in 1956 they were less than half as many). This was because the turnover was exceptionally large and not because the UNR's candidates were exceptionally young, indeed its newcomers tended to be older than most new deputies had been in the past. The reason was largely that both in 1958 and 1962 many of its recruits still came from a Resistance background. The battle between the Fourth and Fifth Republics was mainly fought out within the tiny group of active Resisters.

In one respect the new men arrived by a thoroughly traditional route: in 1958 almost three-quarters of the deputies had been and almost

[18]The classification here is also based on Dogan but differs from that in Table II. It covers the whole Fourth Republic instead of its last Parliament only, and counts engineers and all teachers among the professions (in the Table the former are with business and the elementary schoolteachers among the poor; the 1967 figures are less reliable).

[19]Similarly most women members of Parliament had been Communists, and their numbers dropped from 19 to 6 in the Assembly and from 11 to 5 in the Senate.

[20]From 162 deputies in 1924 to 71 in 1945, 74 in 1958, 52 in 1962 and 48 in 1967.

TABLE II

Social Composition of Parliament in Three Republics (%s)

	Senate incl. overseas, C. of R.			Chamber & Assembly (France only)				
	1939	1955	1959	1936	1956	1958	1962	1967
1. Workers	–	3	2}	13½	13	1½	5	6½
2. Clerks					9	5	8	6½
3. Teachers (elem.)	–	4½	3}	10½	6½	2	4}	14
4. (sec., univ.)					8½	8	6}	
5. Lawyers				20	13	16	11	10
6. Doctors etc.				8	5	12	12	10
7. Journalists				9	4½	5	4	4
8. High Civil Servants	9	10½	9½	3½	4	8	9	9
9. Officers, priests etc.				1	1½	2½	4	2
10. Engineers etc.	2	4½	5	2	4½	6	4	5
11. Managers	3	10	11½	2	5	7	9	5½
12. Businessmen	10½	8½	10	14	10	15½	14½	8
13. Small shopkeepers					6			
14. No occupation	6	–	1					(11)
15. Farmers	15½	20½	24	13½	10	11½	9	7
16. The poor (1–3 above)	–	7½	5	23	29	9	17	19
17. The professions 4–9 above)	62	49	43	42	36	51	46	43
18. Business (10–12 above)	16	23	27	18	19½	29	28	18½
Women	–	3	1½	–	3½	1½	2	1½

two-thirds still were local councillors in their constituencies.[21] These links tended to grow stronger in later years, for many deputies, especially among the younger Gaullists, responded to the early weakness of Parliament by concentrating on local government activity. The mayor of a town of any importance became a much more prominent public figure as the deputy declined, and the member who was also a mayor could both fortify his hold on the constituency by successful administration, and also use his parliamentary status to enhance his prestige in bargaining with firms and ministries in Paris. If he was not yet a mayor he could hope to use the valuable opportunities offered by the developing machinery of regional government to build up a local reputation which might also later enable him to become one. So marked were the attractions of local government that some of the ablest members of the opposition parties chose to devote their main attention to their municipal and regional responsibilities and treat their parliamen-

[21] Local government was even better represented in the Senate.

tary position as an adjunct to their work as mayors.[22] This was much less true of the UNR, and those Gaullist members who made a mark in the Assembly as well-informed and trenchant rapporteurs were very often the same men who were acquiring a reputation in the provinces as successful local administrators.

For both majority and opposition members, the concentration on constituency activities was a highly traditional response to the deputy's new situation. Yet that situation was largely the product of rules designed to upset the traditional patterns of parliamentary behaviour. The paradox was characteristic of the practical working of the new institutions.

(IV) LAW AND HABIT: *plus ça change. . . ?*

Not content with reforming the rules of their streamlined Parliament, the Gaullists also reduced its size. The first National Assembly had 552 members for most of its life, seventy-five fewer than at the end of the Fourth Republic: metropolitan France had 465 deputies instead of 544 (and 598 for a much smaller population in 1936); Algeria, now with the Sahara added, had seventy-one instead of thirty; the four overseas departments had ten, as before; and those few overseas territories which had not become separate States kept six (later seven) members.[23] When Algeria became independent in July 1962 its representatives were instantly removed from parliament by presidential ordinance—a decision which broke a famous precedent (three deputies for the lost departments of Alsace-Lorraine had kept their seats after 1871) and irritated other members, who had not been consulted about the fate of their colleagues. The Assembly was thus reduced to 482 members and the Senate to 274 (from 307 previously and 319 before 1958), of whom 255 sat for metropolitan France. A law of July 1966 added five deputies and nine senators to the third Parliament to represent the growing population of the newly-created departments of the Paris region.[24]

Ever since the second world war the Assembly has had a legal life of up to five years; but no Parliament has lasted more than four and a half. Its normal term expires in April of the fifth year following its

[22]The mayors of Lyons, Lille and Nantes did not stand for Parliament. On those who did see A. Chandernagor, *Un Parlement, pour quoi faire ?* (Paris 1967), pp. 152–4, 162.

[23]All others but Guinea had joined the short-lived Community and were represented in the Community Senate until its suppression in March 1961. For a few weeks in 1959, before its institutions were established, their 24 deputies continued to sit in the National Assembly.

[24]The new departments were allowed to keep PR for the Senate, where the populous departments now have nearly a quarter of the seats (in 1959, with Algeria still represented, they had only a fifth) for 30% of the electorate.

election, though owing to dissolutions and special changes in the law the first post-war election held at the normal time was that of March 1967. The senators serve for nine years, like their predecessors in the Third Republic, and three years longer than in the Fourth; one-third of their members are elected every three years, including all senators from those departments whose turn is due (the list is divided alphabetically).

The conditions of membership were little changed. The minimum age is twenty-three for deputies and thirty-five for senators, who must both have been French citizens for ten years and have fulfilled their military service obligations. Disqualifications include some senior officers and officials in constituencies where they have recently exercised authority; convicts; and persons legally debarred from handling their own finances or exercising their civil rights.[25] Membership is also incompatible with most paid positions in the service of the French or any other State (and with, for example, directing a company contracting for the government):[26] these rules now above all exclude ministers. Members retain much the same privileges as in the past of immunity from arrest or prosecution without the consent of the house to which they belong.[27]

They still sit, according to tradition, around the semi-circular chamber ranged according to their politics from the President's left to his right. The UNR wanted to seat the deputies in the British manner with the majority confronting the opposition, but even their allies resisted and they had to give way. However, they took their revenge for 1951, when the Fourth Republican parties had obliged the Gaullist RPF (furiously protesting like the Poujadists five years later) to sit on the unpopular benches on the far Right—a political position which hardly any French politician willingly admits to occupying. Now the Gaullists could enforce their rejected claim to sit in the centre, and in 1962, with only a shrunken remnant of official Conservatives in the house, the UNR even displaced the Radicals from their usual seats next to the Socialists and sent them to fill up the empty right-wing benches. The scene that followed showed parliamentary traditionalism rampant:

'The members of the Socialist Party call to their colleagues of the Democratic Rally [i.e. Radicals and allies], "Move over, why don't you move over?" The members of the Democratic Rally leave their seats

[25]Jacques Isorni, once Pétain's counsel and later a right-wing deputy, was fined heavily in 1966 for insulting the President of the Republic in a political tract. (There were thirteen cases of this offence in the eighty-odd years before 1958, several hundred since.) This entailed loss of civil rights, and made him ineligible for Parliament for ten years: *Monde*, 24 and 29 Dec. 1966.
[26]Marcel Dassault, whose firm supplies the air force on a colossal scale, is not a 'director' and remains a UNR deputy.
[27]For fuller details see Williams and Harrison, *op. cit.*, pp. 251–4.

and cross to the upper benches in the left-centre. Prolonged applause
from the Socialist and Communist members, standing: *mouvements
divers*. Shouts from the Socialist benches: "Where's the Canon?"
Monsieur Félix Kir joins the members of the Democratic Rally. Loud
applause on the Socialist and Communist benches.'[28]

While the traditional parties were not alone in cherishing customary
practices, they were the most fertile in expedients for preserving them.
When the minimum membership for a recognized parliamentary party
(*groupe*) was raised to thirty in an attempt to stop the proliferation
of tiny groups, the dozen Radicals in the first Assembly promptly
collected enough political neighbours to attain the necessary number:
but the new parliamentary party remained a purely nominal association, splitting into two halves—the Radicals and the rest—for serious
activities.[29] Even with the Gaullists themelves, old habits died hard.
Their constitutional experts, especially Debré, thought the old standing committees were too dominated by pressure groups, which they
hoped to weaken by having fewer committees and broadening their
scope. Under Article 43 of the constitution, consequently, no more
than six may be set up in each house. It was not foreseen that members
would refuse to divide their colleagues into first-rank and second-rank
parliamentarians, and would insist on a committee seat for everyone.[30]
Most of the committees were therefore much bigger than in the past.[31]
   The most striking example of the survival of old habits was the total
breakdown of the attempt to prevent parliamentary absenteeism by
rigid rules. In the past members left their proxies with the party whip
(*boîtier*), and forty or twenty deputies in the chamber often cast four
or five hundred votes for their absent colleagues—though from 1955
personal voting was required whenever the government's life was
officially at stake. Debré had long warred against proxy voting. It
allowed men with heavy responsibilities elsewhere, such as mayors
of great cities, to take on parliamentary duties some of them never
attempted to fulfil, in the hope of strengthening their prestige in their
home town and their influence in Paris. It encouraged Parliament to
sit—and to harass the government—through long summer weeks with-

---

[28]*JO* 13 Dec. 1962, p. 41. Canon Kir, the octogenarian mayor of Dijon, was an
eccentric Conservative who had just allied himself with the Radicals.
   [29]The Democratic Rally, its successor in the second Parliament, had somewhat
more reality.
   [30]Or almost everyone: in the Assembly only members of recognized groups
could elect to the committees, which could then coopt non-party colleagues if
they chose. In the intolerant atmosphere of 1959 these rules allowed the majority
to exclude Communists from all committees as they numbered only ten—too few
to form a group. In later Parliaments they regained their committee places,
which they never lost in the Senate.
   [31]On the old and new standing committees see also below, pp. 62–4.

out many of its members having to inconvenience themselves by attending. It encouraged absenteeism, irresponsibility, and the pervasive illusion that members of the sovereign Assembly could perform several duties at once. The new 'organic laws', drafted under Debré's guidance to supplement the consitution in detail, reflected his views in subjecting proxies to the most drastic restrictions. No member could hold more than one, each had to be notified to the President of the house concerned, and they were allowed only for a very few specified reasons such as illness, serious family trouble or membership of an international assembly. Members who were absent too often were even to forfeit part of their salaries.

These arrangements did not long survive. Absenteeism soon flourished again, worst of all on Fridays (the day for oral questions in the Assembly) but to an unprecedented extent all the time, in committee as well as in the chamber and in party meetings as well as during official business. The only change made by the introduction of new rules and machinery—the deputies now enjoyed electronic voting—was that *boîtiers* had to be younger and more agile men than before, since they were now required to leap up and down the benches switching keys for their absent friends instead of merely putting ballot-papers into a box. Parliamentary camaraderie ensured that after the first few months no one ever suffered from the financial sanctions, and that a couple of dozen members could still cast several hundred votes.[32] If necessary a Gaullist would obligingly cast the Socialist vote against a government bill, while next day a Socialist would return the favour by switching the UNR's keys to defeat his own party's amendment. By the end of the second Parliament a leading journalist could publicly name the three or four assiduous provincial members in each party, contrasting them with the scores who never came to Paris except on Wednesdays and Thursdays in the session, and then looked in only briefly at the Assembly.[33]

French political human nature was as stubborn a plant among ministers as among members of Parliament, as the attempt to separate the two showed. The member who joined the government had to resign his seat, and this penalty would, it was hoped, check the feverish struggle for office which in Gaullist eyes was a major cause of ministerial instability. Every candidate at an election had to stand together with a

---

[32]As in 1963 when about fifty deputies passed the estimates for the ministry of ex-servicemen by 268–192, 'demonstrating, thanks to the electronic system, remarkable dexterity in voting in a few minutes for their absent colleagues': *Monde*, 27–28 Oct. 1963. A year later a budgetary amendment calling for a political amnesty was lost 'in a thin house' by 229–158: *ibid.*, 1–2 Nov. 1964.

[33]P. Viansson-Ponté in *Monde*, 8 July 1966. For the agile *boîtiers*, *ibid.*, 27 Nov. 1963. It would be wrong to assume that the absentees were always devoted to their constituency duties: there were constant complaints that these, too, were neglected.

substitute whose name appeared with his own on the ballot-paper;[34] if the member died or took office his substitute took his place (but was not allowed to oppose his principal at the next general election). A by-election was necessary only if the member voluntarily resigned or if the substitute was also eliminated by death, resignation or acceptance of office. But means were soon found to evade the new rules. It became common, when a prominent minister lost his post, for the substitute to offer to resign the seat and so provoke a by-election which would enable his principal to return—thus frustrating the whole purpose of the change. While these offers were always refused, this probably merely showed the low esteem into which Parliament had fallen. More significant still was the outlook of the ministers in office. At the 1962 election most members of the government stood successfully, including many who had not previously been deputies.[35] Thereafter ministers continued to consider the constituency for which they had been elected as their own and to nurse it attentively. Roger Frey, Jacques Marette and others published their Parisian constituency journals, and local voters approached ministers quite as often as their substitutes to deal with the problems of the district. At election time, provincial ministers pointed—like American senators with seniority—to the benefits their election could bring the constituency as a major reason for returning them to the Parliament they hoped instantly to quit.[36]

Thus the Gaullists' reforming zeal had some ironical results. Some changes worked, but in ways they had not at all expected; others were foiled by the resistance of the politicians, not least of the Gaullists themselves. The constitution-makers did their best to raise the prestige of the Senate—which was to become the stronghold of the opposition. The new electoral law for the Assembly was intended to stabilize the political situation and protect the old parties from too sweeping a change: instead, it helped the UNR to win its unprecedented triumphs. The attempt to improve parliamentary conduct by imposing new rules was a failure, since neither members nor ministers were disposed to respect any provisions of the new order which inconvenienced them-

[34]Except for senators elected by PR, who were chosen on a list system which automatically provided replacements for them. The substitute, usually called *suppléant*, is officially a *remplaçant éventuel*.

[35]In 1960 only half the ministers were former MPs, none of the front rank. But from 1962 there were very few civil service 'technicians'. In the 1967 election only two ministers did not stand; several had become political heavyweights.

[36]In January 1966 Robert Boulin, minister of state for the budget, was triumphantly re-elected at Libourne after his substitute had been killed in a car crash; thanking the voters for the confidence they had showed in President de Gaulle, he remarked that no doubt he had won some personal votes given him gratitude for all he had been able to do for the constituency: *Monde* 11 Jan. 66, cf. *ibid.* 13–14 Feb. 1966.

selves or their colleagues. But where the new arrangements strengthened the government against Parliament, the ministers had a direct
interest in using them to the full. These were the devices by which the
Fifth Republic claimed to restore parliamentary government to France
by enforcing ministerial responsibility to the Assembly, giving members
a more constructive voice in the legislative process, and substituting a
fruitful partnership between cabinet and Parliament for the traditional
guerilla warfare which paralysed the one and discredited the other.
Where the other changes had failed to fulfil their purposes, would these
have better success?

III

Checks on
the Cabinet

(I) PARLIAMENT'S NEW ROLE

John Stuart Mill maintained that a representative assembly was 'radically unfit' to draft the laws and that its 'proper office' was 'to watch and control the government'. Walter Bagehot admitted legislation as an appropriate parliamentary function, but subordinated it to four more important ones: choosing the ministry, expressing the nation's wishes, educating public opinion, and informing the authorities of popular grievances. In the Third and Fourth Republics the French Parliament had sometimes seemed to caricature these views. For while major legislation was hard to carry and often required a grant of special powers to the government, the deliberative functions were all too thoroughly performed. Grievances were so well articulated that action was paralysed, since every offended interest could exercise a veto by withdrawing the votes of its parliamentary sympathizers from the majority. Public opinion learned the views of its political leaders on the major isues confronting the country in debates which were often impressive in their level of argument, but less successful in arriving at constructive solutions. But if the national will received no very clear parliamentary expression, the reason was plain: the divisions within the National Assembly merely reproduced those in the nation, where there was rarely a decisive majority for action on any given topic, still less a majority capable of holding together sufficiently to deal with all problems as a cabinet has to do. In these circumstances the choice of the government, which Bagehot regarded as the primary function of the House of Commons, sometimes seemed in France to have absorbed all the others, not only during the frequent cabinet crises but also for much of the time that a ministry stayed in office.

This was the situation which the makers of the new constitution set out to remedy. The government was to remain responsible to Parliament, but only in the sense that it could at any time be thrown out by a decisive majority against it in the National Assembly. Short of such a majority, hostile, determined and substantial, the ministry was to survive protected from the perpetual pinprickings of the deputies.

The Assembly's opportunities for harassing ministers, as distinct from its right to overthrow them, were therefore carefully limited, and members were prevented from breaking through these barriers by the Constitutional Council, which had to approve their standing orders. But in guarding against the deputies' traditional obsession with Bagehot's primary function, the constitution-makers ran the risk of impeding the operation of the three deliberative functions to which he attached such importance. This danger was accentuated when the Gaullists, already buttressed by the new rules against parliamentary assault, acquired in addition a secure majority in the second National Assembly.

This made the executive as overwhelmingly predominant as the legislature had once been. Parliament was diminished because the main source of policy was not the premier, but a President who was not responsible to it. The government was helped by having almost complete control over the parliamentary timetable. The opposition was hampered by the strict rules limiting the ways of enforcing the government's responsibility to the Assembly; but by far its gravest handicap was the attitude of public opinion. The President, himself subject to direct election by the voters after 1962, could appeal to them over Parliament's head either by authorizing a referendum or by dissolving the Assembly at his own choice. Since the traditional parties were and remained unpopular, de Gaulle first weakened their shaky hold on their followers by well-timed use of the referendum, and then, in October 1962, provoked a challenge in the Assembly which allowed him to dissolve it and win a loyal majority in the new house. Many—though not all—of the critics' complaints arose because of the existence of a government majority which they could neither overcome nor undermine.

(II) THE CONTROL OF PARLIAMENTARY TIME

The first Gaullist objective was to limit the annual period during which the government could be subjected to parliamentary attack. In the Fourth Republic the two houses sat, in principle, all year round and adjournments, unless very short, required the assent of the deputies and could not exceed four months in all. Governments soon found this arrangement inconvenient, and in 1954 regained their old right to send the members on holiday—though they could do so only after the session had lasted seven months, and a majority of the deputies could (like the government itself) always insist on Parliament being recalled. In the Fifth Republic, Gaullist suspicions were plainly expressed in the extension of the recess periods to cover not just the summer but the early months of the year in addition. Under Article 28 of the new constitution there were to be two ordinary sessions: budgetary in the autumn, legislative in the early summer. The former originally ran from the first Tuesday in October to the third Friday in December, and the latter for three months starting on the last Tuesday in April. But in December 1963 the constitution was amended; Parliament could now sit slightly longer in the autumn, for eighty days beginning on 2 October, and in the summer for ninety days from 2 April. Even these limited periods were often interrupted, usually for elections, and experience was soon to show that five and a half months was inconveniently short even for the government to pass its own measures in satisfactory conditions.[1]

Parliament cannot meet in the ordinary recesses, except in special circumstances. In two cases it assembles automatically: under Article 12(3), on the second Tuesday after a general election for a two-week session; and under Article 16(4), if a great emergency leads the President to assume full powers. But otherwise Article 29 provides that special sessions can be called only to discuss a specified agenda, and may not last more than twelve days. As at the end of the Fourth Republic, they can be summoned either by the premier or by a majority of the deputies, but only the premier can recall the house within a month of the last special session.[2] Under Article 30 the President of the Republic, as always in the past, opens and closes special sessions by decree. No one had ever imagined that this provision gave him a right of veto, but in March 1960, when peasant agitation led a majority of the deputies to demand the recall of Parliament, de Gaulle announced that it did; the house, meeting in the ordinary way a month later, rejected a proposal to censure the government for this. Various parties and leaders have called in vain for special sessions on many other occasions, and even the Presidents' Conference, asking for one in January 1962 to debate the Fourth Plan, was told it would not be allowed.[3]

In addition to their ordinary sessions, the first Parliament met six times and the second once. Two of these seven special sessions were unavoidable. In September 1961, Article 16 was in force. The Assembly had met for its ordinary session in April, four days after the emergency was proclaimed by the President, and had chosen to recess at the usual date in July. But under the pressure of renewed peasant agitation its recall was demanded in September, and this time de Gaulle could not prevent it because, when Article 16 is in force, 'Parliament meets

[1]F. Goguel, 'Bilan du travail législatif 1962–1966', Projet 13 (March 1967), p. 297.

[2]This last limitation was due not to the Gaullists but to the CCC, on the motion of Paul Coste-Floret, once rapporteur of the constitution of the Fourth Republic: CCC, p. 99.

[3]Monde, 1 Dec. 1961. See below, p. 44n on other requests, p. 45 on the Presidents' Conference.

automatically'. However, he did warn that it must not attempt to legislate.[4] Another special session became indispensable in March 1962 when the President wanted to hold a referendum ratifying the Evian agreement with the Algerian nationalists which brought the war to an end. Under the constitution this had to be 'proposed' to him by the government when Parliament was sitting; members were therefore recalled for two days. The five other special sessions were all held at the government's choice. Michel Debré called one in January 1959 to present his cabinet to the new Assembly for a vote of confidence.[5] In the following December, when his government had laid the budget before Parliament so late that the members could not otherwise have had the time for discussion to which they were constitutionally entitled, Debré held another special session—which also enabled him to carry his church schools bill. In February 1960, after the 'barricades crisis' in Algiers, he recalled Parliament again for two days to pass a bill conferring special powers on the government. Under Pompidou, only two special sessions were held: one for four days in July 1962, when the house had not finished in time with agricultural legislation which the government had (deliberately) sent them very late; the other in December 1965 to pass a tax reform bill, since the ordinary session had been truncated by the presidential election.[6] When the President began his new term, Pompidou resigned his post according to French constitutional custom; reappointed, he carried out a major reshuffle of his government, but called no special session and held office for three months before meeting Parliament.[7]

In the Third and Fourth Republics, Parliament had always insisted on the right to control its own timetable and oblige the government to

---

[4]This was to lead to a walkout of the opposition members, an attempt to censure the government, and a situation so inconvenient and embarrassing that the President gave up his emergency powers on 30 September. See D. Pickles, *The Fifth French Republic* (2nd ed., London 1963), pp. 151–4, and M. Harrison in 'The French experience of exceptional powers: 1961', *Journal of Politics* 25.1 (Feb. 1963), pp. 149–54.

[5]Until February 1959 the government still had the special powers ratified by the people in the referendum which approved the new constitution. Thus this special session, though it followed a general election, was voluntary and not obligatory. It also allowed the new house to choose its committees and approve provisional standing orders.

[6]On this bill see below, p. 94; on the agriculture bill, G. Rimareix and Y. Tavernier in *RSFP* 13.2 (June 1963), pp. 389–425.

[7]He refused a request to call one for this purpose (and another to debate the Ben Barka scandal). While the refusal was entirely constitutional, it was certainly meant to emphasize that the government was the choice of the President and not of the National Assembly. Contrast the fuss in Britain in 1963 when Sir Alec Douglas-Home, on renouncing his peerage to become prime minister, delayed summoning Parliament for three weeks so that he could fight a by-election and take his seat as soon as the house met.

deliver battle weekly to get its business—even the budget—onto the agenda of the Assembly.[8] Arrangements were always uncertain and members often irresponsible, since they usually preferred to postpone necessary but unpopular measures, such as taxation, to deal with more electorally advantageous ones like higher pensions. During the Fourth Republic, such proposals were often moved by the Communists as an obstructive device, and carried against the government at the last moment. However, the deputies gradually amended standing orders to strengthen the hand of their 'rules committee', the Presidents' Conference; while they clung to the right to reject its proposals, they made it harder and harder to amend them. The Conference consisted of the vice-presidents, the committee chairmen, and all party leaders— who from 1954 wielded a 'card vote' there according to party strength. Thus a government with a majority controlled the Conference, but when its hold on the house was slipping its weakness first became evident there.

In the Fifth Republic matters are very different. The use of Parliament's time is determined primarily by the government, and the opposing parties have no time at all at their disposal.[9] For the official opposition, which in the House of Commons decides the business on twenty-eight days in each session, does not exist in France.[10] Article 48 of the constitution gives priority at one sitting a week to questions, but at all other times to bills introduced or accepted by the government and in the order it chooses. Within these constitutional limits the timetable is decided by the Presidents' Conference and therefore, in the last resort, by the majority. But in practice the Conference rarely votes, and often it serves as a means for conveying the feelings of the house to the government, negotiating compromises, and even persuading ministers to change their minds.[11] Its authority, though restricted, is not unimportant. For it is the Conference which chooses which oral questions the house shall debate and for how long, and these rulings cannot be challenged or even debated by members, except by subterfuge.[12] It also determines what use the house shall make of the time left free by the government, and which private members' bills it shall discuss (here, the Assembly may reject but not amend its proposed agenda). But the time of which the Conference disposes is subject to the goodwill of the government, which can always fill up any spare

[8]See J. Grangé in E. Guichard-Ayoub et al., op. cit., pp. 183–4. For complaints about the old Chamber see Léon Blum, La Réforme gouvernmentale (2nd ed., Paris 1936), pp. 158–9, 171–2.

[9]In France as in Britain the opposition can always get time for a censure motion.

[10]Debré and the UNR wanted majority and opposition members to sit facing one another, but the other parties refused: above, p. 36.

[11]Grangé, loc. cit., pp. 220–2. But cf. Chandernagor, p. 66.

[12]Ibid., p. 224. On oral questions see below, pp. 46–50.

time available—and has even done so occasionally in order to avoid a proposed debate which ministers did not want.[13]

In the last resort, then, the government decides, except on oral question day. Its new authority should have enabled business to be conducted far more efficiently than in the past. But, though the sources of inefficiency and uncertainty are different in the Fifth Republic, the faults themselves have not disappeared: ministers today often use their wide discretion almost as ineptly as the deputies did, but with less excuse. In June 1961 the government agreed very reluctantly to a debate on Algeria, but changed its mind half a dozen times in a week on when the debate was to be. In 1963 René Pleven, an ex-premier and a very moderate opponent, complained bitterly of 'empty trough periods followed by weeks of overwork . . . our working conditions deserve all the criticisms that today's majority brought against the functioning of the Assemblies of the Fourth Republic'. Three years later another moderate, the parliamentary leader of MRP, was repeating exactly the same complaints.[14]

(III) QUESTIONS AND INQUIRIES

Whatever the government's sins in its conduct of business, there is one sector of parliamentary time with which it cannot interfere: oral question day. Oral questions were conceived of by Debré as the principal means by which, short of the heavy artillery of a vote of censure, the Assembly could carry out its function of criticizing the government.[15] In past regimes the great weapon of the critics had been the interpellation, a motion which summoned the government to explain its policy on any question great or small and was sanctioned by a vote expressing, or denying, the house's confidence in the government. In the Third Republic interpellations were the occasion for the fall of

[13]For an example see below, p. 87 (and Grangé, loc. cit., p. 239; cf. Chandernagor, p. 59). The government might hesitate to use this power if the houses chose to sit on a Monday or Saturday to discuss private members' business—as they could, but never do.

[14]Pleven wrote in his local paper, quoted Monde 11–12 August 1963. The MRP leader, Pierre Abelin, was also particularly indignant that a debate on agricultural policy in the Common Market had been fixed to coincide with the meeting of the Council of Europe to which 24 deputies belonged: JO 5 May 1966, pp. 1096–7. The author went to Paris to attend the 1961 debate—only to find it was over. There are repeated criticisms of the arrangement of business in the Revue du droit public et de la science politique (hereafter RDP), whose regular parliamentary critic, Léo Hamon, is a professor, ex-senator and prominent Gaullist. The President of the Assembly, Jacques Chaban-Delmas, has frequently voiced the indignation of members of all parties: e.g. JO 26 July 1963, p. 4602; 20 Dec. 1963, p. 8020; 21 Oct. 1964, p. 3508; 30 June 1965, p. 2794.

[15]As in Britain, written questions are very numerous and often informative, but of little political significance. See however, M. Ameller, Les questions instrument de contrôle parlementaire (Paris 1964), pp. 99–112.

most governments, but in the Fourth they were kept in check and were rarely fatal to a cabinet. But the critics could still harass ministers by motions attacking them on their most vulnerable points, wearing them down by a succession of minor defeats in the 'Friday guerilla' until they had been weakened sufficiently for the final onslaught. This Debré was determined to prevent. He encouraged oral questions (which are rather like adjournment debates in the House of Commons) and considered them as opposition time, not subject to interference from the government; but he would not tolerate voting on them.[16] When the Parliament of the Fifth Republic met for the first time in 1959, this problem caused violent controversy and was partly responsible for the resignation of two ministers. At first the Assembly adopted standing orders permitting motions which could be voted on, and during the brief period they were authorized the new deputies used them as irresponsibly as their predecessors.[17] But then the standing orders were referred to the Constitutional Council.[18] More rigid even than Debré, it ruled that all resolutions were unconstitutional unless they were purely internal to the Assembly (on its accounts, etc.) or specifically authorized by the constitution, like censure and impeachment motions. The politicians were therefore confined, as Debré had intended, to the oral question as their main day-to-day weapon.

Oral questions can be 'with debate' or without. To the latter the minister replies, and his questioner is then allowed five minutes to comment; on the former, speeches can be longer, from a quarter to half an hour. The Presidents' Conference decides into which category a question falls and whether and when it shall be debated—nowadays almost always along with others on the same subject.[19] During the first Assembly about half the oral questions with debate were answered, and virtually all those without.[20] But, despite Debré's hopes, questions have never played the role that they do in Britain. Opposition and majority members alike chose, especially in the early years, to use these opportunities only for the airing of minor constituency grievances; in

[16]There is no vote at the end of an adjournment debate in the Commons either.

[17]See below, p. 98. The senators were no better: in the same month they called for the restoration of ex-servicemen's bonuses by 210 votes to 0. Cf. C. Roig in Guichard-Ayoub et al., op. cit., p. 102.

[18]It was the CCC which had proposed, without opposition, that the standing orders of the two houses should automatically be referred to the Council; CCC, p. 75. (The government draft had merely authorized the President of each house to refer them if he wished.) The mover of this proposal himself became a member of the Council.

[19]This makes for more sensible discussion but it sometimes leads to long delays. In June 1966 the Assembly debated eight oral questions on higher education, one of which had been put down (by a Socialist) in 1964.

[20]Grangé, loc. cit., pp. 252–3. On the second Parliament see Monde, 15 Feb. 1967.

the first Assembly only four out of 149 oral questions with debate concerned either of the major political problems, Algeria and foreign policy. The government did nothing to encourage members to take questions seriously; even ministers who answered them often arranged for a colleague to read out the departmental brief on a subject in which he had neither interest nor knowledge.[21] Moreover, oral questions day in the Assembly was Friday, when members were hurrying off to their constituencies: on one memorable Friday, November 22, 1963, André Malraux addressed an audience of eight deputies, soon reduced to five and finally to three.[22] In the Senate, however, question-time was put to better use: the opposition had abler spokesmen there, its question day was Tuesday, and the upper house had less pressure on its time, especially early in the session when little legislation was coming up from the Assembly. Thus in the summer session of 1963 the Senate spent two-fifths of its time on oral questions which were often on major political topics (including fifteen out of seventy-seven on Algeria or foreign policy).[23]

As opposition time, oral question day was a total failure in the Assembly—though not in the Senate. The opposition itself was responsible for its ineffective and unimaginative use of its opportunities, but the blame must in part be shared. First, in the Assembly the Presidents' Conference did not treat oral question day as an occasion to give priority to the opposition, but continued instead the old Fourth Republican tradition of allotting a roughly proportionate number of questions to each party.[24] Then, the ministers were often obstructive. While they showed no particular zeal for replying quickly to questions they did not like, most of their delays were doubtless due to simple inertia—though Debré himself in a circular in September 1961 asked them to give special attention to answering questions by government supporters.[25] But finally, there was a political problem more serious than

[21]Ameller, pp. 166–7; and below, p. 50. This abuse happened less on oral questions with debate; and deputies, as well as ministers, were often absent when their questions were called.

[22]The questions were not all on his own ministry. On another occasion when there were only six deputies present for the last question, its author pointed out that the house had risen at 6 a.m. that day, his committee had met at 9.30 in the morning, and after a long afternoon sitting the house was to discuss the supplementary estimates next day: R. Vivien, *JO* 18 July 1963, p. 4297; cf. Hamon and Emeri, *RDP* 79.6 (Nov. 1963), p. 1162.

[23]Grangé, p. 266.

[24]But in the Senate the parties most hostile to the government, with 42% of the seats, asked 76% of the questions in the first Parliament: *ibid.*, p. 269. In the Assembly questions without debate from the opposition (which were rarely more political than the others) averaged 35% of the total in six sessions from spring 1960 to spring 1963: Ameller, pp. 185–8.

[25]An opposition senator read it to the house: *JO* (*Sénat*), 5 June 1962, p. 418. By telling the Presidents' Conference which minister is available, the government

ministerial delay or favouritism. It was that opposition time which is ultimately controlled by the representatives of the majority is a contradiction in terms.

It is not suggested that questions from opposition parties are systematically or even frequently suppressed: on the contrary, those that are put down are generally called for debate.[26] But it is maintained that no opposition can do its job properly unless it can decide for itself when to exploit a tactical opportunity to inflict the greatest possible embarrassment or damage on the government. And this, from time to time, it can be and is prevented from doing. For example, when the first talks with the Algerian nationalists were held in June 1960, the leader of the European settler deputies from Algeria put down an oral question for debate which was refused time by the Presidents' Conference—in which the left-wing opposition agreed with the Gaullist majority that it was highly inopportune.[27] Nor have such incidents occurred only in wartime, or only in moments of crisis. In May 1963, when the government was already unpopular owing to the miners' strike, a crucial by-election took place in a wine-growing region. Generous time was allotted to the numerous opposition questions on the wine-growers' grievances, but nearly all of it was after the by-election was over.[28] In June the majority allowed a debate on the way the government used and misused the official radio and television, but gave it far less time than the opposition wished. But in 1964 when François Mitterrand asked a question on the premier's role in the government, Pompidou rightly thought he could turn it to his own advantage and called a debate at the first possible moment.

The government, then, is not merely secure against defeat so long as its majority remains loyal. It is not merely protected by the new rules of procedure against harassing tactics and damaging votes on minor points. It is even able to impede opposition attempts to seize public attention at the right moment and so make their debating criticisms effective—for, as every parliamentarian knows, in politics timing is

can often in effect choose which questions to answer: Chandernagor (a Socialist deputy), *op. cit.*, pp. 66–7.

[26]But not always. When de Gaulle was met by riots at Djibouti in August 1966, Mitterrand put down a question which, *inter alia*, reminded the government it had never answered his earlier question on the situation in the overseas territories—dated 19 December 1963 (*sic*).

[27]*JO* 30 June 1960, pp. 1596–7.

[28]Wine-growers were again annoyed in 1965, when a Socialist leader complained that sixteen questions on their problems had remained unanswered for eight months—and repeated his complaint five months later: *JO* 13 May 1965, p. 1318; 2 June, p. 1730; 17 June, p. 2200; 2 Oct., pp. 3277–8; 17 Nov., pp. 4715–6. When a Communist protested that her questions on textile workers' grievances had been neglected for sixteen months a Gaullist reproached her with 'propaganda': *JO* 19 May 1965, p. 1432.

D

often crucial. No doubt the majority representatives use their power to block criticism only when they think their opponents are behaving irresponsibly and demagogically. Unfortunately, every majority is always predisposed to believe that every opposition is behaving in this way—and there is no sanction against similar conduct on the part of the majority.

While Debré's intention to establish a genuine opposition time was thus frustrated, oral question day could still have served a useful purpose if members or ministers had treated it more seriously. Everyone was rather ashamed of the failure, and in December 1963 an attempt at reform was made. The legislation and standing orders committee persuaded the Assembly to change question-time from Friday afternoon to a mid-week morning sitting—with an hour of the afternoon added so as to keep the same total time. Through its UNR rapporteur the committee also urged strict enforcement of the standing order requiring ministers to answer their own questions; the house narrowly rejected an opposition amendment allowing them to send a colleague only if the questioner consented. The Constitutional Council then stepped in and ruled both reforms unconstitutional.[29] In spite of this setback, a better-led opposition has used the procedure somewhat more vigorously since 1964, with major debates arising from oral questions on the premier's role in the government, on foreign aid, education, social security and (six months late) on the Ben Barka scandal. But while question day is no longer exclusively an occasion for airing petty constituency grievances, it is still far from becoming a recognized period when the government's critics freely choose the time and topic for their attack.

Committees are another means by which Parliament can 'watch and control the government'. There are six ordinary standing committees with a mainly legislative role, dealt with in the next chapter. Most of them at times, and the foreign affairs and defence committees nearly always, had acted in the past as vigilant critics of administration and policy as well as drafters of legislation; they were therefore another object of Gaullist suspicion.[30] Parliament can also set up committees

[29]The new time was invalid because the constitution authorized only a single sitting for questions: if members chose a morning they must lose an hour a week since no part of another sitting could be added to make up the time. The standing order forbidding ministers to send substitutes was invalidated because, the government being one entity, the premier could delegate anyone he chose to speak for it and the house must not interfere with his choice. (Yet the Council had approved this same standing order in 1959, and the UNR President of the Assembly had then used it successfully to stop the abuse for a time: Grangé, *loc. cit.*, p. 168.) See *JO* 19 December 1963, pp. 7989–92, 2 April 1964, pp. 604–5; *Monde*, 30 Jan. 1964; *RDP* 80–1 (Jan. 1964), pp. 95–100.

[30]Early in 1962, as OAS terrorism was spreading in Algeria, the government decided to withdraw two divisions from that country. The Assembly's defence

of inquiry into matters of public concern (as the House of Commons did over the Marconi scandal and the Labour opposition wanted to do over Profumo). In the past such committees in France, like those on the Stavisky affair in the Third Republic and on the 'scandal of the generals' in the Fourth, were a good means of attracting publicity but a very bad way of arriving at the truth about the matters in dispute. In the Fifth they are severely restricted, limited in their duration to four months (after which they cannot be reconstituted for twelve), and in their scope to exclude any question that is *sub judice*.[31] Elected by majority vote, they could never be very effective opposition instruments, and few have been proposed and none set up for a political purpose.[32] On one terrible occasion in October 1961, when the Paris police were accused of drowning dozens of Algerian Moslem demonstrators in the Seine, Gaston Defferre moved in the Senate for a committee of inquiry. The minister of the interior, Roger Frey, refused altogether at first, then agreed provided nationalist terrorism was also investigated, and finally set up a judicial tribunal: this staved off any other inquiry by making the matter *sub judice,* but its results (if there were any) were never revealed to the public.[33] Again in 1966 the government successfully resisted all demands for a parliamentary or other inquiry into the Ben Barka scandal.

(IV) CONFIDENCE AND CENSURE

In making it difficult for the opposition to challenge the government by motions or embarrass it by awkward committee inquiries, the constitution-makers of the Fifth Republic were guarding against the unhappy experiences of previous regimes, when repeated attacks on minor points had threatened the cabinet with defeat if it did not

committee, a stronghold of the right-wing opposition, despatched a mission to report on this decision: but one member, the extremist Colonel Thomazo, was stopped at the airport and his colleagues refused to go without him. (A month later all MPs were barred from Algeria.)

[31]The Constitutional Council curiously ruled in 1966 that the four months must be consecutive, though sessions last only three: L. Hamon and C. Courvoisier in *RDP* 82.2 (March 1967), pp. 300–1.

[32]The Assembly established one, in December 1960 on state aid to the cinema industry, and the Senate two: in 1962 on the management of the national theatres, and in April 1966 on the educational selection process in schools. This last committee heard much evidence and in December 1966, by oral question, provoked a major Senate debate. The stopped six in the Presidents' Conference second Assembly: Chandernagor, pp. 78–9, 105–6.

[33]Four months later eight more victims, Communist demonstrators against OAS terrorism, were crushed by a police charge against the closed gates of the Charonne metro station. This time Frey blamed first the Communist party, then OAS terrorists disguised as policemen.

make them matters of confidence and with the rapid exhaustion of the members' goodwill if it did. Far less defensible was the decision made in 1958 that the government might refuse a vote in the house on declarations of policy made to Parliament on its own initiative. This extraordinary reluctance to permit the members to 'evolve and express clearly the political choices before the nation' (as de Gaulle once officially described their function) apparently rests on yet another of Michel Debré's many misunderstandings of British government, for he once explained to the deputies that British MPs very rarely vote.[34] The government has almost always denied an opportunity to vote on its own declarations of policy, and Debré often tried to refuse even a debate in the Assembly (he could not prevent one in the Senate). Debré's government made twenty-seven such policy declarations: to the Senate ten, and to the Assembly seventeen: six on foreign affairs, five on Algeria, four on economic and social questions, one on education, and one on the police repression of the Algerian demonstrators in October 1961. On eight no debate was allowed, only a five-minute reply by one speaker—but on the schools question the President of the Assembly would not choose between several different oppositions so no one answered at all, while on the police repression he permitted a UNR member to reply for the opposition! On the nine other declarations there was a notably dull debate, for with no vote coming, the government did not bother, as it must in legislative discussions, to try to convince the deputies.[35] Pompidou's government made fewer declarations of policy—only six to the Assembly and none to the Senate— but allowed debates on all of them. Two were on economic and social questions, two on education, and two on foreign affairs. On the first, in June 1962, the entire opposition walked out of the house in protest when the government would allow no vote on its European policy.[36]

The constitution-makers thus succeeded in their object. A vote can be forced on government policy, as distinct from legislation, only when the cabinet's very existence is at stake. Such a challenge may come about on the initiative of either the opposition or the government itself. First, the prime minister can ask the Assembly (not the Senate) to vote by an ordinary majority its confidence in the cabinet's programme or on a declaration of general policy. Each premier has sought the Assembly's confidence twice, once on his programme when first appoin-

---

[34]JO 26 May 1959, p. 559. In fact there are three times as many divisions in the House of Commons as in the new National Assembly: in an average year about 200 at Westminster and 65 in Paris (800 under the Fourth Republic). From October 1963 to April 1966, MPs voted as often as deputies had since the new regime began. (De Gaulle's comment was made in his first formal message to Parliament: JO 15 Jan. 1959, p. 24.)

[35]On this foregoing paragraph see P. Avril, Le Régime politique de la Vᵉ République (Paris 1964), pp. 110-7, 293.

[36]This was the occasion of the declaration of the 293: below, p. 100.

ted and again, a few months later, on his general policy. Debré won his first vote in January 1959, and his second in October after de Gaulle had promised self-determination to Algeria—insisting with character-istic rigour that the vote was on his policy as a whole and not just on Algeria, which would have been tactically more favourable to him. Pompidou, winning an unimpressive majority in April 1962, resigned after being censured in October, was reappointed, and sought a vote of confidence from the new house after the dissolution and the Gaullist election victory.[37]

The government can also make the acceptance of a bill a matter of confidence. If so, the bill is passed unless the opposition puts down a censure motion within twenty-four hours and finds a majority of the whole house (not just those voting) to carry it. A censure motion can also be proposed by opposition members on their own initiative. Under Article 49, either type must be signed by a tenth of the deputies and cannot be voted on until forty-eight hours after its introduction; only those voting for the motion are counted and a majority of the whole house is required to pass it, so that absentees and abstainers help the government. If the initiative is the opposition's, the signatories of the motion cannot propose another that session, but they can do so if they were responding to a government demand for confidence on a bill.[38]

Nine votes of censure were proposed in the first Assembly, and two in the second. The left-wing parties—ten Communists, forty-five Socialists and about thirty Radicals and allies—voted for all but one of the first nine. As 277 votes were needed to carry a censure motion up to June 1962, when the Algerian deputies disappeared, and about 240 after that date, the Left needed at first nearly 200 allies and at the end over 150 if it was to turn out the government. Five of the first nine motions were against bills which the government had made matters of confidence, three were at the initiative of the Left opposition, and one came from the extreme Right. Four dealt with defence, Europe or foreign policy generally, three were on agriculture (though in one case this was not specifically stated) and one on the budget; the last victorious motion was exclusively on the working of the constitution, but this was also an issue in all the others. The signatories were once, over Algeria, drawn exclusively from the far Right and three times, on domestic issues, from the Socialists and Radicals (the Communists were too few by themselves and too unwelcome to the others). MRP

[37]When the third Assembly met in April 1967 he made a declaration of general policy but did not seek a vote.
[38]This restriction may hamper one opposition party but it cannot help the government escape defeat. If there were a hostile majority in the house, there would be enough signatories for five censure motions a session, or one every two or three weeks. The restrictions on censure motions were invented not by Debré but by the ex-Fourth Republican ministers in de Gaulle's cabinet.

and Conservatives also signed the foreign and defence motions, and all the opposition parties except Communists were represented among those signing the final motion. The two censures in the second Assembly were on agriculture and on the French withdrawal from NATO. Both were signed by the moderate Left, and the former by MRP also. The Communists did not vote for the NATO censure.[39]

TABLE III

Confidence and censure votes in two National Assemblies

No.	Date	PM	Type	Subject	Initiative	Signatories	Opp.	Votes Gov.	Abs.
1.	Jan.'59	Debré	Confid.	Programme	Gov.		56	453	29
2.	Oct.'59	Debré	Confid.	General policy (Algeria)	Gov.		23	441	88
3.	Nov.'59	Debré	Both	Budget	Gov.	Soc, Rad.	109		
4.	May.'60	Debré	Censure	Not calling Parl. (agric.)	Opp.	Soc, Rad.	122		
5.	Oct.'60	Debré	Both	Nuclear deterrent	Gov.	Soc, Rad, Con.	207		
6.	Nov.'60	Debré	Both	Nuclear deterrent	Gov.	Soc, Rad, Con.	214		
7.	Dec.'60	Debré	Both	Nuclear deterrent	Gov.	Soc, Rad, Con.	215		
8.	Dec.'61	Debré	Censure	Unspecified (but agric.)	Opp.	Soc, Rad.	199		
9.	Apr.'62	Pompi	Confid.	Programme	Gov.		128	259	119
10.	Jun.'62	Pompi	Censure	Algeria	Opp.	E. Right	113		
11.	Jul.'62	Pompi	Both	Nuclear deterrent	Gov.	Soc, Rad, MRP, Con.	206		
12.	Jul.'62	Pompi	Confid.	Nuclear deterrent	Gov.	—	—		
13.	Jul.'62	Pompi	Confid.	Nuclear deterrent	Gov.	—	—		
14.	Oct.'62	Pompi	Censure	Constitution	Opp.	All-party	280		
				New National Assembly					
15.	Dec.'62	Pompi	Confid.	General policy	Gov.		116	268	69
16.	Oct.'64	Pompi	Censure	Agriculture	Opp.	Soc, RD, CD.	209		
17.	Apr.'66	Pompi	Censure	NATO	Opp.	Soc, RD.	137		

As a means of strengthening the cabinet the censure rules had some success. In the early days at least, the atmosphere of the censure

[39]In the third Assembly the government made its special powers bill (above, p. 28) a matter of confidence. A censure motion signed by the Communists and the Federation (non-Communist Left) attracted centre support and 236 votes, eight short of a majority, in May 1967.

debates and the balance of speeches were often far more adverse than the final vote: MRP, for instance, usually criticised the government but did not vote against it. In 1960 a procedural vote against the nuclear deterrent bill was lost by 213 to 264 with 40 abstaining, a government majority of fifty-one; the censure motions which followed on the same bill still had just as many supporters but the asbtentions were concealed, so that the opposition was sixty short of success and the government's majority therefore looked like 120. By covering up such cracks in the majority, the government is made to appear stronger than it really is.[40]

The most serious criticism of the new French Parliament was that its creators, in their determination to prevent it spending all its time making and unmaking ministries—Bagehot's first function—had hampered it in carrying out those three deliberative functions which Bagehot had regarded as next in importance. The opinion of the nation is not always expressed, or ever declared by a vote, unless the government so chooses or its life is at stake. Grievances can be put forward, but the government's facilities for resistance are so great, and the cost is so small when there is not even a vote recorded, that ministers have little incentive to attend to complaints unless an election is approaching. The opposition parties and their leaders have lamentably failed to exploit the opportunities they still enjoy; the majority is generally loyal, and any waverings within it are usually hidden from the public eye. The proceedings of Parliament therefore offer no surprises and little interest, particularly since the government prefers to make concessions, if at all, in private. So, while the 'bull-fight' attractions of the Assembly have fortunately disappeared, no alternative spectacle has taken their place. Very rarely on a great occasion like the debate on the Plan in November 1965, or on the withdrawal from NATO in April 1966, Parliament will attract some public attention and demonstrate that French politicians have not lost their talent—and that the Gaullist leaders can well hold their own with their predecessors. But such events are infrequent. The weakness of Parliament has diminished public interest in it, and the low standing of politicians in the country contributes to their apathy and lack of self-confidence.

Parliament was bound to attract less attention as long as major policy was determined by an exceptional personality independent of its control, and often only executed by the responsible ministers who appeared before it. But while the atrophy of its deliberative functions has harmed it in public esteem, the constitution-makers have enjoyed far more success in their reform of the legislative process.

[40]Had the same rules applied in the House of Commons during the 1963 Profumo debate, the Conservatives' votes would not have been counted and, with their abstentions concealed, Macmillan's premiership would not have been shaken.

Streamlined Legislation

(I) THE DOMAIN OF THE LAW

Under previous regimes Parliament had passed a large number of bills and considered a great many more. The government had a hard struggle to get its business through amid the flood of private members' legislation, and conscientious rapporteurs and committees, who spent much time on bills which never reached the statute book or even the floor of the house, sometimes had too little left to consider adequately those that finally passed. These measures, even the government's, could be amended out of all recognition in committee, and it was the committee's rapporteurs who piloted them through the house. The government was not even allowed to move amendments in its own right, and had to find a friendly deputy to do so instead. As new amendments and even whole new drafts of the bill could be freely proposed on the floor, debate was often poorly organized and results incoherent. The upper house could revise badly drafted legislation, but it was so obstructive in the Third Republic that it was reduced to a subordinate role in the Fourth. While its decline removed one great obstacle to legislation, those that remained in the Assembly were quite sufficient to impede the progress of any major measure which offended an important interest; even if it survived in committee, it was likely to provoke the defection of marginal votes from an always fragile majority, and so bring down the government. As a rule, such controversial bills could pass into law only if the members broke the spirit of the constitution by temporarily abdicating their legislative powers to the government itself. Indeed, time was hard to find even for quite uncontentious measures. In practice, therefore, the legislative omnipotence of the National Assembly incited it to disperse its energies under unsatisfactory conditions over an enormous mass of trivial detail, without enabling it to deal effectively with any major reform.

The new regime reacted against this state of affairs. Parliament's legislative function was limited by new rules which changed its procedure; imposed financial checks on its members, who could not propose to raise expenditure or lower revenue;[1] and—most far-reaching of all—prohibited it from legislating at all except on matters where it was specifically authorized to do so. Hitherto Parliament had been altogether unfettered and the government had been limited. Where no law applied, the courts had allowed the executive to act on its own initiative—under what in Britain would be called prerogative powers—for three purposes: the maintenance of public order, which in France is always broadly defined; the organization of public services; and, subject to some limitations after 1946, the government of colonies. But now Article 34 of the new constitution lays down boundaries defined according to the subject-matter. It specifies a 'domain of the law' within which alone Parliament can legislate and where normally the government cannot; everything else forms the 'domain of regulations' where the government can make rules with which Pariament cannot interfere. The boundaries are protected by Articles 37 and 41, which prevent Parliament from encroaching, but they may be temporarily shifted under Article 38, which allows the government to encroach with Parliament's consent. The domain of the law embraces three areas: first, those covered by the organic laws specified in various Articles of the constitution, such as the budget, or the detailed regulation of the various constitutional organs; secondly, those subjects on which Parliament may lay down 'rules', i.e. legislate in detail—for example, civil liberties, the electoral system, nationalization and denationalization of industries; thirdly, subjects like education, national defence, or social security, where Parliament may legislate only about 'fundamental principles'.

The domain of regulations is wide, since it embraces everything else, but it covers the less important aspects of public life. Indeed, it is a sign of the triviality of members' preoccupations in the Fourth Republic that nine-tenths of the bills introduced in its last year, and half those passed, would have fallen into the domain of regulations. At the start of the new regime the number of private members' bills brought in was cut from 800 to 200 a year, mainly because of the limits set by Article 34.[2] The average annual number of bills reaching the statute book dropped from 225 in the earlier and 175 in the later years of the Fourth Republic to seventy-three and 109 in the first two Parliaments of the Fifth,[3] but the political difference was smaller than the numerical, since the eliminated bills were mostly minor ones which used to pass through Parliament with little or no debate.

Disputes about the boundaries between the domain of the law and

[1]See below, pp. 81-2.

[2]L. Hamon and C. Cotteret in *RDP* 76.3 (May 1960), pp. 656-7. A quarter of those eliminated were out of order under the new financial rules.

[3]Unpublished paper by F. Goguel, read at Princeton, N.J. on 16 April 1966, p. 6; his article in *Projet* 13 (March 1967), p. 284.

the domain of regulations may become subject to adjudication by two different authorities. Bills can be referred to the Constitutional Council; lawsuits between the citizen and the State go ultimately to the *Conseil d'Etat*—which, in another capacity, is also the government's legal adviser on the drafting of all bills. Here its views are not binding, but have great weight because of its dual function. Thus in 1964 it advised that the government could not by decree allow the police to endorse driving licences on the spot, as this was a matter for legislation; the government could have disregarded this opinion only at the risk of losing lawsuits coming to the *Conseil* in its judicial capacity.[4] The working of the system can be seen in the social security field. Patients have to pay 20 per cent of their medical bills unless this amount is waived or cut. The government would like to tighten the conditions of waiver, but the Patients' Federation opposes this. A decree introduced in 1958 was annulled by the *Conseil d'Etat* in 1961, revised and reintroduced next year, but again annulled because, affecting the fundamental principles of social security, it was held to be a matter for the law.[5]

The Constitutional Council operates at the legislative stage. Contrary to a common view which had some plausibility in the early days, it has often ruled against the government. Indeed its decisions have tended not to restrict Parliament's scope, but on the whole to broaden it by attenuating the distinction between those subjects on which Parliament can lay down 'rules' and those on which it must confine itself to 'fundamental principles'. Thus, while the objective of legislation is for Parliament to decide, the government can choose the method of reaching it—except where the method would determine or frustrate the objective aimed at. For example, Parliament may decide the qualifications for a proxy vote—but not the administrative procedures required to claim it. It may prescribe that local authorities should have representatives on the Paris Transport Authority—but not how many (though the government cannot so reduce the number as to destroy the principle). It can pass a law setting up a new type of criminal court to operate in Paris, Lyons and Marseilles; but the extension of these courts to other towns would be a matter for governmental decision. Although in all these cases Parliament is entitled to lay down rules, the Council has limited the detail into which it may enter by insisting that the rules must be settled and important. Conversely, in the areas where Parliament can deal only with 'fundamental principles' and a strict construction might have greatly hampered it, the Council's interpretation has been broad. The 'fundamental principles' of social

[4]*Monde* 21 Feb. 1964. But the *Conseil's* advice sometimes restricts Parliament's rights, as when it had some clauses removed from the bill extending social security to the self-employed: see *JO* 9 June 1966, p. 1848.
[5]*Monde* 27 Nov. 1963.

security, for instance, have been construed to extend far beyond the principles governing the system as a whole.[6] In theory its jurisdiction might conflict with that of the *Conseil d'Etat*;[7] but this seems not to have occurred so far.

The Constitutional Council firmly guards the boundary between legislative and executive spheres against any encroachment from the parliamentary side. Its authority depends on different articles of the constitution according to when it is invoked: during the legislative process (41), after that process is completed (61), or even after the bill has finally been promulgated (37). The government can claim that a private member's bill or amendment is out of order because it falls outside the 'domain of the law'.[8] Its claim can be challenged by the President of the house concerned and taken to the Constitutional Council. The President of the Senate has been much less reluctant to use this right than his Assembly colleague—a leader of the UNR.[9] Then under Article 61 the Council can be asked by the Presidents of the Republic or of either house, or by the premier, to rule on the constitutionality of a bill which has passed through all stages but has not yet been promulgated. Such rulings are few and are almost always sought by the government, but Monnerville referred the bill for direct election of the President in order to challenge the constitutionality of the procedure; the Council prudently declared itself incompetent to pronounce on a bill adopted by the sovereign people at a referendum. Finally, even when a measure has reached the statute book, the government can use Article 37 for second thoughts. If it wishes to override a pre-1958 act which dealt with matters outside what has now become the domain of the law, it has to seek (but need not take) the advice of

[6] Among these are, for example: free choice of doctor; freedom of prescribing; separate schemes for farm-workers, railwaymen, and others. But the Council has also included the principles of operation of these separate schemes, and those determining the qualifications for different types of benefit (e.g. it is a 'fundamental principle' of social security that only those drawing a family allowance can benefit from a housing allowance). Rates of contribution or benefit can be altered by the government, but it could not frustrate the objects of the system by reducing a benefit to a purely nominal amount. In practice it clears changes informally with the Council before enforcing them.

[7] A government, against which the *Conseil d'Etat* had decided a case by ruling that a matter fell within the domain of law, could then bring in a bill and refer it to the Constitutional Council in the hope of reversing that verdict.

[8] Or within an area delegated to the government temporarily under Article 38: below, p. 72.

[9] In 1961 Jacques Chaban-Delmas, fearing a rebuff from the Council, allowed the government to win without seeking a ruling when it opposed an amendment dealing with Parliament's representation on a fund for aid to the states of the Community. Conversely a year before, when Gaston Monnerville challenged the government over an amendment to an agricultural investment bill, it was the latter which gave way without appealing to the Council. See *JO* 8 Nov. 1960, pp. 3327–8; *JO* (*Sénat*) 6 July 1960, pp. 717–8, cf. *ibid.*, 3 Dec. 1964, p. 2119.

the *Conseil d'Etat* before making regulations which supersede the act. But if it wishes to override a Fifth Republican law on the same grounds, it needs the consent of the Constitutional Council.[10]

While the government is fully armed against parliamentary encroachment, it need not use its safeguards. On the church schools bill in December 1959, the government yielded to its majority, who doubted its pro-clerical zeal, and allowed the Assembly to encroach far into the domain of regulations. On the agriculture act of 1960 it accepted detailed amendments on the price-fixing machinery.[11] Sometimes ministers may disagree with their supporters—or with one another—about how to use their wide discretion; over the companies act of 1964, the ministry of justice drafted a comprehensive bill—but the prime minister's office eliminated half the clauses, which fell within the domain of regulations.[12] When the Left Gaullist Louis Vallon proposed to allow a parliamentary committee to scrutinize the accounts of the Bank of France (and of some semi-public companies), the minister of finance successfully challenged the amendment before the Constitutional Council 'to avoid a question of this importance falling within the domain of the law'.[13]

The government thus enjoys a wide discretion. But Parliament cannot refer a decree to the Council for a ruling.[14] Members cannot bring a dispute to its notice by introducing a bill, for the government is master of their agenda. The President of either house can refer a bill to the Council, but he is unlikely to challenge a government decision to allow Parliament its say. In the last resort, here as elsewhere, the members have only one final remedy for their frustrations: a motion of censure.[15] But while the executive's own sphere is thoroughly walled off against parliamentary encroachment, it is still allowed under Article 38 to encroach on the legislative domain as it so often did in the past.[16]

---

[10]The government sought 23 such rulings in the second Parliament; it won 10, lost 3 wholly and 8 in part; on 2 the Council declared itself not competent: Goguel in *Projet*, *loc. cit.*, p. 289.

[11]It warned that they might be changed under Article 37; and they remained a dead letter: Goguel at Princeton, *loc. cit.*, p. 22. Contrast below, pp. 91–2 & n.

[12]*Monde* 21 May 1964. Cf. Avril, *Régime*, p. 26 & n.

[13]*JO* 9 Nov. 1964, p. 5208. But the government is not always restrictive: see below, p. 91.

[14]However, members could challenge it in the *Conseil d'Etat*, which recognized their *locus standi* in Canal's case in 1962 (below, p. 74n).

[15]Article 34 itself does envisage its terms being clarified and completed (*précisées et complétées*) by an organic law: but the meaning of 'completed' is not clear, the organic law must apparently be once for all, and its constitutionality will have to be affirmed by the Constitutional Council under Article 6. Would the Council allow it to broaden Parliament's sphere?

[16]See below, pp. 72–5.

(II) BILLS IN THE NATIONAL ASSEMBLY

Within the sphere in which it is still able to legislate, Parliament is further limited by the procedural advantages which the government now enjoys. At the first stage, the constitution allows private members to introduce bills (Article 39), but gives priority to measures brought in or taken up by the government (Article 48); and the Assembly's standing orders guard against any attempt to obstruct. The share of private members' bills among the measures passed into law therefore dropped sharply, from nearly 30 per cent in the Fourth Republic to about 7 per cent in the first Parliament of the Fifth; in the second Parliament the proportion climbed back to 11 per cent.[17] Nor are the crude numbers an adequate political index. Some government bills are inspired by private members' proposals; others deal with areas where only the government can or does legislate—finance, defence, customs treaties.[18] And the political importance of private members' bills is easily exaggerated. Hampered by the financial restrictions imported from British parliamentary practice, their authors still frequently concentrate on trivia: the depredations of wild boars attract the attention of many eastern deputies, while politicians of all parties from Nord want cock-fighting legalized. Many private members' bills are brought in with the sponsor's election address rather than the statute book in mind, and 70 per cent are never reported to the house.[19]

In the first Parliament, opposition members had as good a chance as majority ones of seeing their proposals debated and even adopted by the government (without which, as in Britain, their hope of success was small). But in the second, there were constant and apparently well-founded complaints that the cabinet favoured the bills introduced by its supporters.[20] Its right of priority enables it to block bills it dislikes, though—given the character of most private members' proposals—this

[17]First Parliament: Grangé, *loc. cit.*, pp. 242–5. Second: *Monde*, 15 Feb. 1967. Of 51 bills passed in 1959, only one was a private member's bill; but in 1965, 9 out of 72 were: Chandernagor, p. 58, for annual figures. The first Parliament passed 19, the second 53: Goguel in *Projet, loc. cit.*, p. 285.

[18]Leaving these areas out of account, private members' bills would be 15% of those passed up to 1962, instead of only 7% (and would be 30% of those debated): Grangé, pp. 242, 261–2.

[19]Very few of these are ruled out of order under Article 34. Among the few was a UNR deputy's bill to oblige every village *mairie* to display the President's portrait (ruled out on a report from an ex-UNR member turned right-wing extremist). For one old-style politician and the bills he promoted see M. Harrison in *Political Studies* 7.2 (June 1959), pp. 147–56 (on the man), and Grangé, pp. 265–6 (on the measures).

[20]For the first Parliament see *ibid.*, pp. 267–9; for the second, Avril, *Régime* (2nd ed., Paris 1967), p. 381 & n.—of 23 bills brought in by deputies and passed in or before 1965, 19 had sponsors from the majority, 1 from the opposition and 3 from both.

need not imply much discrimination betwen parties.[21] At first the government's tactlessness provoked even the UNR President of the Assembly to protest at its behaving as 'an autocrat arrogating itself full powers the better to abuse them, especially by preventing, through its control of the agenda, the discussion of any private member's bill and indeed of any subject desired by the representatives of the nation'.[22] After this outburst the government acted less rigidly in the Assembly. In the Senate it is weaker, for the flow of government legislation is harder to regulate and the opposition controls the Presidents' Conference: in 1964 the Senate was able to vote by 215 to 0 a private member's bill—for an amnesty to all political offenders—which the government succeeded in keeping off the floor of the Assembly.

In the Fourth Republic, the committees of the house were the main agency for slaughtering the more trivial and demagogic private members' bills (with the Presidents' Conference in reserve to deal with those which slipped through a committee). Bills that survived these hurdles—including the government's—were often completely reshaped and then piloted through the house not by their author, but by the committee's rapporteur. The nineteen compact and specialized standing committees of the Assembly were proportionately representative of the parties but disproportionately of pressure-groups, since they were dominated by members with a personal, professional or electoral interest in their subject. They were therefore an object of deep suspicion to the Gaullist constitution-makers, who took several steps to weaken them. Through its control of the agenda the government can now call up a bill before the committee has reported; it very rarely does so, but the power guarantees it against obstruction. The house now debates the government's draft of its own bills, to which the committee presents amendments (but private members' bills are still discussed on the committee's draft). Debré would have liked to abolish the regular standing committees altogether, and to send most bills to special committees set up *ad hoc*; but in the end Article 43 merely limited the number of standing committees to six in each house. It is still at the committee stage that bills are most seriously examined, and they always take longer to pass through committee in the house where they were introduced than to shuttle between the houses until their terms are agreed.

The six standing committees are formed by proportional representation: of all members in the Senate, of official party groups in the Assembly—where a member resigning from his party loses his

---

[21] A typical victim was the bill to promote the use of the Breton language, proposed in 1960 and never discussed. Majority members suffer too: Chandernagor, p. 59.

[22] *JO* 6 July 1961, p. 1480.

committee place, as he did at the end of the Fourth Republic.[23] Since all senators and almost all deputies sit on a committee, these bodies are much larger—and therefore much less cohesive—than they used to be: in the Assembly the finance and foreign affairs committees each have sixty members and the other four ninety.[24] At first some of them overcame this drawback (thus frustrating the intentions of the constitution-makers) by setting up sub-committees under another name. For example, the production, trade and exchange committee of the Assembly had four vice-chairmen who each presided over a 'working group' in which membership was continuous and the parties were represented proportionately just as in the old days; the new agricultural working group, with its forty-six (instead of forty-four) members, still attracted all the peasant deputies—and the former chairman of the old agriculture committee still presided over it. Before long, indeed, even ministers were appearing before these sub-committees for hearings.[25] But as parliamentary absenteeism spread, an older practice revived: increasingly committee meetings were attended only by members interested in the bill to be discussed. This had always happened in the legislation committee, with its immensely varied agenda, and soon it became common in the others as well. Sub-committees therefore became less and less necessary.

Ministers took the Senate's committees more seriously than the Assembly's. But even in the upper house critics maintained that they did less work and held less through hearings than in the past.[26] Absenteeism was a perennial complaint. Opposition members often stayed away because they could make no headway against a disciplined majority. But Gaullists too were often absent—so that François Mitterrand was once chosen to report on a bill he violently opposed,

[23]So Léon Delbecque, the main organizer of the riots in Algiers which destroyed the Fourth Republic, became chairman of the cultural and social affairs committee in the new Assembly but was ousted from it when he left the UNR in October 1959 (above, p. 25). On the exclusion of Communists in that Assembly see above, p. 37n.

[24]The legislation and defence committees have had 90 since 1958; Production, and Cultural and Social Affairs, had 120 each until the Algerian deputies left in July 1962. In the Senate two committees have 35 members each, three 44, and one 68 (since July 1962). Before 1958 all committees had 44 members in the Assembly and 33 in the Senate. On their working in 1959 see C. Roig, *loc. cit.*, pp. 60–2, 94–9.

[25]But many Gaullists continued to dislike them; some ministers would never go and others would not send their officials.

[26]E.g. Senator Armengaud in *Monde*, 9 April 1964; cf. Chandernagor, p. 93. But the committees were sometimes better than their reputation. In the autumn session of 1966, for example, the Assembly's rapporteurs of the defence and housing budgets made effective criticisms and won important concessions; the rapporteur of a bill setting up new joint conurbation authorities spent two days in each area consulting the local councillors; and the 'pill committee' (below, p. 65n) heard many distinguised medical witnesses.

to prolong the life of the military court trying security cases. Even without such incidents, the committees remained fortresses of the government's critics. In October 1960 the deputies' dislike of the nuclear deterrent bill was foreshadowed by critical or hostile reports from three committees. Just as in the old days, the defence committee mobilized the critics of the 1963 bill on conscientious objectors, and the 1965 measure organizing military service; the finance committee in 1961 favoured raising civil service salaries but opposed all the new taxes proposed to finance the increase; the production committee in 1963 welcomed the stabilization plan but attacked cuts in the agricultural estimates.

These bad old habits did less damage than in the past, for the Gaullists maintained their discipline whenever the government stood firm.[27] Moreover, the size of the new committees made it harder than before for a few pressure-group spokesmen to win a majority by packing a meeting or by skilful log-rolling. This still remained easier than it should have been, since members attended only for bills that interested them; but on the whole the big new standing committees proved less vulnerable to pressure-group activity than the special committees which the constitution-makers had expected to supersede them. For these had only thirty members, whose interests were likely to be concentrated rather than diverse. For example, in June 1961 thirty-one farming deputies called for a special committee on the government's bill for disposing of the milk surplus; won their point against both government and finance committee; placed eleven of their number on the special committee, which reported—unanimously—against imposing any levy on milk producers to help pay the cost; and thus obliged the government to withdraw its bill in order to kill the committee.

This was not the only reason why special committees were rarely used. Either the government or the house can ask for one to be set up, and in 1958 it was assumed that this would be done for any bill which overlapped, as major measures normally do, the sphere of several standing committees. But the regular committees disliked losing their jurisdiction;[28] and before long even Debré lost his enthusiasm for special committees, since they take time to establish and more to get their members working together, and—unlike their regular counterparts—are always an unknown quantity. With both ministers and standing committees disliking them, the first Assembly set up only ten and the Senate eight; in the second Parliament there were five and four in the two houses. Only one was on a measure of first-class

[27] See below, pp. 79, 82, 90, 94-5, 105, 119.
[28] If three committees ask within three weeks to discuss a bill, a special committee has to be set up. They never do, for the third committee does not ask until three weeks have gone by. Cf. Roig, loc. cit., p. 97.

importance, the agriculture act of 1962; again the special committee of the Assembly proved far more tender to conservative propertied interests than was the government, and carried the house with it. Most special committees were on such highly technical subjects as urban development, river pollution, or the pensions code, and here they enabled specialists from several standing committees to be brought together on a complicated bill, and often—especially in the Senate—proved highly successful.[29]

In the past, Parliament made many bad decisions about its own time-table. Now, however, the government decided in what order bills should be placed on the agenda, and ministers in their turn frequently used their new and unlimited authority with little consideration or foresight. Complaints were endless, especially in the upper house. The government presented its bills late in the day and asked Parliament to rush them through at an excessive pace. At budget time in particular the Gaullists resumed the night sittings which they had so vigorously criticized in the past. The autumn session was overloaded as the government tried to squeeze extra business into the time allotted for the estimates, while in the summer the Senate, especially, was under-employed at the start and frantically rushed at the end. In 1964 it was asked to sit for a legislative purpose only ten times in April and May, but fifteen times in June; for six weeks the government did not bring forward a technical measure on river pollution, which the committee had ready at the start of the session—yet at the end of the session its rapporteur was asked to draft six reports in ten days.[30] Nor were protests confined to the upper house. In June 1966 a bill to extend social security to self-employed workers was rushed through under urgency procedure. It was not referred for advice to the Economic Council, and was put on the Assembly's agenda less than a week after being distributed. Only a few roneo'd copies were available for the social affairs committee, and the finance committee had no chance to produce a written report. The house had insufficient

[29]The controversial 'bill for the Pill', proposed by some UNR members (and opposed by others) to repeal part of the 1920 law prohibiting the practice of or propaganda for contraception, was sent to a special committee in 1966. An unsuccessful motion for a special committee sometimes enabled the opposition to force a debate and vote which the government did not want, as on the amnesty for Algerian war offences in December 1966. In April 1967 the government agreed to a special committee on its demand for delegated powers (above, p. 28n).

[30]JO (Sénat) 30 June 1964, pp. 946–7, 966. The rapporteur (Pierre Marcilhacy) asked the prime minister 'to allow Parliament to work at the start of a session instead of leaving us to . . . twiddle our thumbs for a month and a half only to inundate us with work in the last week'. For a similar protest by a UNR member (Michel Boscher) the day before see JO, p. 2316. In the previous summer session the Senate had sat: in the second week for one day, less than 90 minutes; in the eighth week on five days, averaging six hours each; in the thirteenth week, on all seven days: Hamon & Emeri, RDP 79.6 (Nov. 1963), pp. 1160 ff.

E

time to discuss the 145 amendments presented. The minister argued that after all the long discussions on the subject, the time for action had now come. But it was a majority member who complained that 'this shows once again how little account the government takes of Parliament's efforts'.[31]

During the discussion on the floor, the government is again far better placed than it was in the past. The minister pilots his own draft of the bill, and he can rule out of order any amendment which has not previously been discussed in committee—though this right is rarely used and many debates have been reduced to chaos by a proliferation of new amendments in the house.[32] He can even withdraw the measure altogether if he dislikes the course of the debate.[33] But his most useful procedural weapon is the 'package vote' authorized by Article 44 (para. 3) of the constitution. This device, which was invented in the last decadent days of the Fourth Republic, allows the government to call for a single vote on *'tout ou partie'* of a draft. Interpreted to mean 'all *and* part', it permits one single vote to be taken on the whole bill, modified if the government so agrees, without a separate vote on any of the politically difficult clauses or amendments. In the Third and Fourth Republics the government could carry the unpopular parts of its proposals only by making them matters of confidence, which gradually drained away its political credit. Now it can avoid this danger by linking the fate of the entire measure with that of the difficult item. In the new regime the package vote obliges members to pronounce on a given clause or amendment in the context of the bill as a whole, while the vote of confidence, now reserved for more solemn occasions, obliges them to pronounce on a whole bill in the context of their attitude to the government in power.[34]

In the first Parliament of the Fifth Republic, where the government had no reliable majority and needed every advantage, there were forty package votes—an average of six a session. But under Pompidou, who disposed of a loyal majority which should have allowed him to dispense

[31]*JO* 9 June 1966, pp. 1827, 1838, 1848. (The minister, Jeanneney, had never sat in Parliament.)

[32]It is not a complete dead letter, and was used successfully against an amendment to a bill on the debts of refugees from North Africa: *JO* 24 June 1966, pp. 2339-40. But in the same month a private member's bill on farm tenancies was amended by 'changes so muddled that they defy analysis': *Monde*, 5-6 June 1966.

[33]A married women's property bill passed the Assembly in 1961, recognizing the wife's rights subject to exceptions; the Senate gave priority to the husband subject to exceptions; the deputies (against their own committee) restored the wife—and the government withdrew the bill in the middle of the debate. In the end it passed unanimously—four years later.

[34]See below, p. 72. The government spokesman before the CCC defended the package vote as a means of reducing the number of confidence votes: *CCC*, p. 116.

with his cruder weapons, Article 44 was used far more than under Debré. In the corresponding period of the new Assembly, up to June 1966, there were 118 package votes—an average of fifteen a session. With fewer political difficulties, the government thus used the package vote more freely; it also did so much more harshly.[35] When the Gaullists allowed Parliament to vote on the national Plan before it came into operation, they reasonably required that it be accepted or rejected as a whole, without log-rolling amendments. But most package votes are called for purely tactical purposes on contentious subjects.[36]

The device is not particularly useful against the thoroughgoing opponents of the government, who challenge its measures as a whole and whose amendments rarely find favour among ministerial supporters. Occasionally it can be useful against critics on the majority benches themselves, as in June 1965 when a bill to strengthen works committees in factories had a much warmer welcome from most of the opposition than from some government supporters. But often the deputies of the majority accept and even welcome it;[37] for it saves them the embarrassment of having to vote openly for unpopular clauses which the ministers are determined to defend, or against attractive amendments which their leaders obstinately resist. It is used less against destructive criticism, which could easily be beaten off without it, than against precisely those amendments which are sufficiently reasonable—or demagogic—to tempt supporters of the government. Thus, while it shelters the loyal followers and does little real harm to the extreme opponents of the government, it is particularly detested by the moderate critics for 'introducing between government and Parliament the methods and style of the referendum'.[38] One of the three occasions on which the whole opposition has walked out of the house in protest was in December 1964, when the government used Article 44 against attempts to extend the amnesty to all 'political' offenders.[39] Giscard d'Estaing, who had used the package vote freely as minister of finance,

[35]Avril, *Régime*, 2nd ed., pp. 382, 384. In *RDP* 81.3 (June 1965), pp. 410, 419–20 he compares the government's use of the package vote in the four years of the first Assembly and in the first two years of the second. It put through its own draft of a bill without allowing any amendment only twice in the early period but five times in the later. It accepted a few amendments, then called for a package vote to stop any more, seven and eighteen times in the two periods. It used Article 44 in these ways on the first reading (which stifles debate) four and six times respectively. (*Monde* 15 Feb. 1967 found only 19 package votes in the first Parliament and only 67 in the second.)

[36]Two-fifths are on the budget; the next commonest subject is agriculture: Avril, *loc. cit.*, pp. 411–2.

[37]Cf. Goguel in *Projet* 13 (March 1967), p. 288.

[38]André Colin, chairman of the MRP senators: *JO* (*Sénat*) 23 July 1963, p. 1825. See also below, p. 109.

[39]On the other occasions see above, pp. 44n., 52.

promptly condemned the government's excessive fondness for it when he left office and wanted to differentiate himself from his former colleagues and from the UNR.[40]

(III) THE SECOND CHAMBER

Once through the National Assembly, bills go to the Senate. In the Third Republic, disputed bills went through a *navette* (shuttle) between the two houses until agreement was reached—which might be never—and the Senate often buried bills it disliked, simply by never reporting them out of committee. The Fourth Republic guarded against such obstruction by allowing the deputies to override the upper house very quickly and easily—and therefore to ignore it altogether as they often did.[41] In 1954 the senators obtained a limited delaying power which ensured that their voice was heard; this compromise worked very well for the short period it operated. In 1958 the new regime, under Article 45, replaced it with a new arrangement by which the government gains complete control of the *navette*. After two readings on a bill (but only one if they declare it urgent) ministers may, but need not, take three steps. First, they may call a conference committee (*commission mixte paritaire*) of seven members from each house.[42] Secondly, if it reaches agreement, they may submit its draft to Parliament together with only those amendments which they have themselves introduced or accepted. Thirdly, if it disagrees or if its draft is rejected in either house, the government may (but again need not) ask the Assembly for a final decision. The deputies can then pass into law either their own draft, with or without all or some of the Senate's amendments, or the conference committee's draft, with any amendments accepted by the government. Ministers can thus use either house against the other, relying (as it was thought in 1958) on the presumably friendly Senate to block any undesirable proposals from the turbulent and irresponsible deputies, who would have no redress except with the government's consent—and overcoming with the help of the National Assembly any unexpected recalcitrance by the Senate. In addition, along with the package vote and the vote of confidence, these provisions allowed the government in an extreme case to impose its own wishes even though both houses disliked them—provided always that the Assembly had no majority willing to turn the government out. While this was done very rarely indeed, the possibility

[40]*Monde*, 7 May 1966. Yet despite the package vote, each year the Assembly accepted half the amendments which deputies proposed: *Monde*, 15 Feb. 1967.

[41]But a clear majority of all senators could be overruled only by a clear majority of all deputies, which was hard to find.

[42]If not, they can either kill the bill by keeping it off the agenda, or simply continue the *navette*.

enhanced the government's bargaining strength in more normal trans-
actions.

Only the government can start the machinery for speeding up the
navette by calling a conference committee. As in Washington, the
chairmen of the main committees of the two houses act as its chairman
and vice-chairman, and the members are normally well qualified technically. In practice there are twenty-eight, as each full member has a
substitute who sits and can speak (but can vote only if his principal is
away). To minimize *esprit de corps*, voting is secret. The government
has no representative, so a conference committee sometimes reaches a
compromise without knowing exactly what ministers will or will not
accept.[43]

In the first Parliament each house usually chose its conferees in
rough proportion to party strengths.[44] This always gave the opposition
parties a majority, since among the senators they were six to one,
and among the deputies either two against five or three against four.
Consequently, in the second Parliament, except on quite minor bills,
the Assembly chose only representatives of the majority—even when
members of other parties had voted for the bill in question. The Senate
preferred not to follow suit, and in protest at the Assembly's behaviour
it usually continued to elect one UNR member; but he often refused
to sit, and occasionally, on matters of acute controversy such as the
municipal electoral law or the bill reorganizing broadcasting, he was
not given the chance. If the National Assembly sends only supporters
and the Senate only opponents of the government, the chances of dead-
lock in the conference committee are obviously maximized—which
suits the deputies who, with the government's help, can always win.
But the senators were often conciliatory, and conference committees
brought forward an agreed draft surprisingly frequently: eleven out
of thirteen did in the first Parliament, and thirty-six out of forty-seven
in the second. The upper house, however, resented the Gaullist tactics
and under Pompidou it became increasingly common for the whole
Senate to reject a compromise draft accepted by its conferees. In 1964–
1966 conference committees agreed on twenty-six bills out of thirty-
five (and on part of another): of the agreed reports the Assembly
rejected one and the Senate seven, though the former could and did
override the latter. But even when one house refused a conference
report, the agreed amendments in it were often kept in the final act—
a sensible solution not expected (though not excluded) when the system
was invented.

The new arrangements worked admirably where the bills concerned

[43]For a full but early account of conference committees see H. Trnka in
RDP 79.3 (May 1963), pp. 477–534.
[44]Except on non-political measures, and on the bill creating the District of
Paris where members from the capital were given favoured treatment.

were not at the centre of the political conflict. In these cases the conference committees reached agreement and the two houses accepted their drafts far more quickly than they could have done through the clumsy process of successive readings in each house; for example, a bill on rural leaseholds had been in *navette* from 1956 until it went to conference in 1963.[45] Even on controversial matters the machinery sometimes assisted the process of conciliation. Thus in December 1963 the Senate wrote wrecking amendments into the next year's budget, and then rejected its own version because the UNR senators joined the Left in voting against it. Each house sent only conferees representing its majority view, but the seven opposition senators selected were moderate men. The government made a few concessions, they made more, and the Senate voted a conference committee draft leaning strongly towards the Assembly's version. Similarly in 1964 the upper house first amended and then rejected a major bill reforming the administration of the Paris region. The conference committee unanimously approved a draft incorporating many senatorial amendments; the minister of the interior accepted it and came to the Luxembourg Palace to defend it; and although the opposition protested that their conferees had conceded far too much, their colleagues passed the new version.

These arrangements ensured that on matters of political controversy the Assembly could always be sure of getting its own way. With the Gaullists in control of one house and the opposition of the other, conflicts were frequent—especially after 1962 when the government had a secure majority in the Assembly and bad relations with the Senate. The deputies used their final power to override the senators on only 1 per cent of bills in the latter years of the Fourth Republic, under 2 per cent in the first Parliament of the Fifth. But in the second Parliament the proportion rose to 5 per cent, with a peak of 9 per cent in 1965, the presidential election year.[46] Most politically important measures passed in this Parliament were voted against the will of the Senate;[47] for it had no power to obstruct and little opportunity to persuade, since the government regarded it as committed to opposing all Gaullist policies. Its influence on major policy or on important economic and administrative measures was therefore small. But it played an important part in the legislative process on purely technical and legal bills, where its expertise was welcome and its conservative views might be acceptable to the deputies—if not to ministers.

Even on political measures, an apparent difference between the houses sometimes masked a real clash between a reforming government and conservative feeling in Parliament generally. Defenders of property

[45]On this rather technical bill the Assembly chose one opposition conferee.
[46]Goguel, *loc. cit.*, pp. 286, 287n.
[47]The law on the Paris area was the chief exception.

in both houses whittled down the government's agriculture bill of 1962 so severely that, when the conference committee agreed on a much modified draft, the minister decided it was the best he could get and used the package vote to protect it from still further erosion. In 1964 the UNR parliamentary party brought in a private member's bill on agricultural contracts, which the two houses passed in different versions.[48] The conference committee unanimously agreed on a draft which leaned to the Senate side. The minister of agriculture felt the government had too little control over the funds involved, but the rural pressure-groups protested at his amendment, the Right opposed it, the UNR rapporteur warned that the Senate would never accept it, and it was lost. The conference committee draft then went through against the opposition of the Left. In this minor instance, then, deputies and senators worked together through the conference to impose their views on the government.

Far more frequently, however, the government has gained from the system. For on bills it dislikes it can block the machinery: it can refuse to set up a conference committee at all, to send their draft to Parliament, or to give the Assembly the last word. But on bills that it wants, it can greatly speed up legislative procedure, which is now far more rapid than in the past. Of the twenty most controversial bills in the first Parliament, ten were passed within a month and six more within three; only one took more than a year.[49] Besides gaining time, the government can play off one house against the other, and can even—provided the Assembly does not censure it—impose its own amendments to the conference report. By the end of 1964 it had done this on four budgets, two supplementary estimates and two ordinary bills, one dealing with strikes and the other with broadcasting.[50]

On matters of political importance, therefore, the practice of bicameralism bears little relation to the theory. On paper, the two houses differ about a bill and the government can then set up concilia-tion machinery. If the aim of the conference is to resolve a disagree-ment between the houses, the Senate and the opposition are logical in arguing that the minorities in each house should be represented. But on matters of heated controversy the real purpose is quite different: it is either to enable government and majority, working together, to overcome a recalcitrant senatorial opposition, or even to allow the government (always provided the majority is unwilling to turn it out) to defeat its critics anywhere in Parliament.

[48]On its origin see below, p. 106; and on the 1962 act, Rimareix and Tavernier, *loc. cit.*

[49]Grangé, pp. 199, 256–7. Twenty bills: 13 which went to conference and 7 needing six or more readings in each house.

[50]See below, pp. 90, 92.

(IV) LAWS NOT VOTED BY PARLIAMENT

Nothing prevents the government using the conference machinery in conjunction with its most drastic weapon of all, the vote of confidence procedure. As explained in Chapter III, a bill which the government declares to be a matter of confidence passes the Assembly automatically unless a majority of the entire membership is found to carry a motion of censure. It was pointed out in 1958 that by combining these two procedures the government could pass into law a bill for which neither house had voted; a government spokesman admitted that this could happen in theory but called it 'morally and politically impossible'.[51] Yet two years later Debré's government carried in this way the bill to create an independent nuclear deterrent, which the Senate twice rejected and the Assembly passed three times only because censure motions failed to win a majority.[52] In the first Parliament the government used the question of confidence seven times, almost always on the deterrent.[53] It never did so in the second Parliament where its majority was secure.

Finally, there are three ways by which legislation can acquire legal force without going through Parliament at all: by authority of the government, of the President, or of the electorate. The government under Article 38 can seek from Parliament a special and temporary grant of legislative powers to deal with a specified subject. Essential under the old regimes when it was difficult to carry major measures against serious parliamentary resistance, this has less justification in the new when the procedure is less cumbrous, the government far stronger and, as it has turned out, the majority more reliable. There are safeguards: a time-limit must be prescribed, ordinances under Article 38 must be approved in cabinet (not just by one minister) after the *Conseil d'Etat* has been consulted, and they lapse unless a ratifying bill is laid before Parliament by a date specified in the enabling act. But the government can cheat, for while the bill must be 'laid' it need not be passed or even debated.[54] There is a mild penalty for cheating, since acts made under these special powers can be challenged in the administrative courts as *ultra vires* as long as Parliament has not ratified them: only after ratification do they acquire the force of law.

[51]Quoted *JO* 22 Nov. 1960, p. 3957, by François Valentin.

[52]For reasons discussed at pp. 25–6, 99–100. De Gaulle (but not Debré) even contemplated invoking Article 16 if the censure passed: L. Terrenoire (then a minister) *De Gaulle et l'Algérie* (Paris 1964), p. 196.

[53]See Table II, p. 34. The seventh case was on the budget (essentially the ministry of pensions estimates) at the end of 1959. The special powers bill of May 1967 (above, p. 54) was made a matter of confidence early in the third Parliament.

[54]See below, pp. 87–9.

Under Article 38 the first Parliament passed four enabling acts, and the second three. The first was voted after the 'barricades crisis' in Algiers, and gave the government special powers to safeguard the State and the constitution, and to pacify and administer Algeria. These powers were limited to a year and the ratification bill had to be laid two months later, by April 1, 1961; they were granted only to the existing government, and ordinances under them had to be signed by the existing President of the Republic; they were to lapse if Parliament were dissolved; and the government promised not to use them to restrict public liberties or trade union rights, set up special courts, or carry out administrative reforms in France itself. Under this enabling act thirty ordinances were passed, dealing with the judicial code and procedure, the security of the State, and the administration of Algeria. Only one seemed to fall outside its terms: this prolonged the legal life of a State holding company for newspaper printing-presses. But several, though *intra vires,* were potentially dangerous.[55] As the ratification bill was never debated, these regulations did not acquire the force of law and at least one was successfully challenged in the administrative courts.[56] A second major enabling act dealt with alcoholism and other 'social scourges'; it is discussed in Chapter VI. A third authorized the government to alter existing laws about the allotment of housing and the grant of professional and social security qualifications, so as to facilitate the resettlement of refugees from North Africa. Three more (not used before 1967) empowered it to bring French law into line with the directives of the European Economic Community; since ordinances made under these are to carry out the terms of an international treaty, Parliament's right to ratify them can only be nominal. The seventh allowed the government to implement the decision of the Somalis if they voted for independence in the referendum of March 1967.[57]

In addition to these delegations of legislative power to the government under Article 38, President de Gaulle in the summer of 1961 took eighteen 'decisions' under the emergency powers he had assumed by invoking Article 16 of the constitution. He was also (under what constitutional authority is far from clear) granted powers by referendum in April 1962 to bring into force the Evian agreements which ended the Algerian war. This last bill included none of the usual safeguards. One of the fifty-three ordinances made under it removed

[55]One sent *all* cases arising out of the Algerian war to military courts. Another forbade anyone *accused* of a crime to stand at the next local elections; it was aimed at Pierre Lagaillarde, leader of the barricades rising, but his wife stood in his place and won.

[56]By Colonel Trinquier, an extremist officer even by Algerian standards, who left intending to command Tshombe's gendarmerie in Katanga. The regulation would have deprived him of French nationality. See *Monde,* 6, 7 and 8 Feb. 1961.

[57]They did not. For the May 1967 enabling bill see above, p. 28.

the Algerian members from Parliament.[58] Another abolished the special court, originally set up under Article 16, which had failed to sentence to death the rebellious General Salan, and established instead a military court from which there was no appeal. In October 1962 this was ruled *ultra vires* by the *Conseil d'Etat*;[59] but in January 1963 Parliament ratified all the ordinances and thus revived the military court.

The third form of non-parliamentary legislation is the referendum under Article 11, which has been used so far only on three occasions: in January 1961 on self-determination and provisional institutions for Algeria, in April 1962 on the Evian agreements, and in October 1962 for direct election of the President of the Republic by popular vote (although—or because—in normal procedure amendments to the constitution have to go through Parliament). Altogether between 1959 and 1966 a total of 117 legislative acts (or 17 per cent of the total number) were not debated in Parliament: three laws voted by referendum; the President's decisions under Article 16 and ordinances under the Evian bill; and the governmental ordinances under the Article 38 enabling acts. But with only two exceptions the delegations of legislative power have arisen either out of crises due to the Algerian war, or as an uncontroversial way of amending the law to implement the Common Market treaties. From 1962 to 1967 the law-making power in the Fifth Republic again rested with Parliament.

The fact remains that Parliament has lost its old right of legislative self-determination. The National Assembly can be confronted with a vote of confidence—in which the rules make it harder to defeat the government, whose power of dissolution makes the deputies less disposed to do so. The Senate can be overcome without difficulty or great delay through the conference procedure. Both houses can occasionally be by-passed, with their own consent under Article 38, even without it by a referendum. None of these changes means that Parliament is in practice less able to legislate than it used to be. On the contrary, it could rarely put to positive use the power it theoretically enjoyed in the past, since with weak governments and unstable majorities the motive force was far too feeble and the opportunities for obstruction were far too many. The Gaullists had some ground for regarding Parliament as an obstacle to major reforms rather than a source of them. Here the new regime has transformed the situation. The limits imposed on Parliament's scope give it a far better chance of working effectively within the broad sphere in which it is still competent. While private members' bills are fewer, some useful ones

[58]Above, p. 35.
[59]On appeal by André Canal, an OAS leader sentenced to death by this court. Five senators also challenged the decree; the *Conseil d'Etat* recognized their *locus standi*.

TABLE IV

Authorisations of legislative powers to the executive

No.	Date	Authority	Subject	Period	Ratif. bill by	No. of ordinances*
1.	4. 2.60	Art. 38	Government of Algeria etc.	12 months	1. 4.61	30
2.	30. 7.60	Art. 38	'Social scourges' (alcoholism etc.)	4 months	15.12.60	7
3.	23. 4.61	Art. 16 (Pres.)	Emergency powers	(renounced 30.9.61)	—	18
4.	26.12.61	Art. 38	Resettling refugees	4 months to 23.4.62	2 months later	6
5.	13. 4.62	Art. 11 (Pres.)	Enforcing Evian agreements	while relevant	—	53
6.	8. 8.62	Art. 38	EEC agric. policy (Agric. Act, cl. 24)	to 30.6.63	each ordinance within 3 months	0
7.	14.12.64	Art. 38	Enforcing Treaty of Rome	to 1.1.66	1. 4.66	0
8.	6. 7.66	Art. 38	Same (prolonged)	to 1.1.70	1. 4.70	?
9.	22.12.66	Art. 38	Evacuating Somaliland if it chose independence	4 months or till Parl. debates	1.12.67	N/A

*To December 1966.

still reach the statute book, though they may need government assistance to do so. The government can pass its own measures into law in reasonable time, but not without affording opportunity for criticism in committee and on the floor—though the government can use the package vote procedure not merely to keep its bill intact, but to enable its supporters to escape whatever distasteful responsibilities this might otherwise entail. The upper house is able to persuade, but its inability to coerce weakens its efforts at persuasion. Parliament's real influence is largely exerted behind the scenes, for ministers are often receptive to informal pressure from their majority.[60] The normal legislative process today can cope, without suppressing parliamentary criticism, with many more important measures than it could usually accommodate in the past. Here if not elsewhere the constitution-makers have largely achieved their aim, and between them Gaullist rules and Gaullist majorities have brought about in Paris a balance of power not unlike that which exists at Westminster. The real benefits of this new situation would have been more widely recognized if the new masters had not—here as elsewhere—so often abused the advantages that they gained from their reforms. It was over the annual budget that the problems which confronted them over ordinary laws were met in the most acute form, for this was the most regular, most essential and most politically difficult legislation of all.

[60]See below, Chapter VII.

V

The Power
of the Purse

(I) THE BUDGET

The budget has always played an even greater part in French politics than in British. It was the great legislative event of the parliamentary year, the chief occasion for criticizing government policy and administration, and an opportunity for aggrieved interests to press their case on a ministry which needed every vote it could get. So crucial was it to the survival of governments that it provoked half the votes of confidence in the Fourth Republic (before decolonization had become the central political issue, the proportion was two-thirds). Because the budget fulfilled all these parliamentary functions, it absorbed so much of members' time and energy that they were hampered in all their other activities; because it suffered long delays in Parliament, the administration had to operate unsatisfactorily on monthly 'provisional twelfths' which sometimes authorized over half the year's expenditure. A new procedure, introduced in 1956, might have remedied many weaknesses, and saved the house's time by concentrating on matters which its finance committee considered contentious.[1] But it had only one year of proper trial before the Fourth Republic collapsed.

The constitution of 1958 did not impair Parliament's right to reject the budget, but imposed strict limits on the time it could take to make up its mind. The National Assembly had to vote on it within forty days, otherwise it went automatically to the Senate which had two weeks to consider it. If Parliament's decision had not been reached within seventy days, the government could bring in the budget by ordinance.[2] The procedure was fully defined by an organic law, issued by the government early in 1959 under the unlimited legislative powers it enjoyed for the transitional period, and therefore

[1] See Williams, *Crisis and Compromise*, pp. 268–9.
[2] It could not do so, of course, if the decision was to reject the government's proposals. And if these were laid late, Parliament had extra time beyond the normal sessions to consider them. The Senate's two weeks was double its 1956 allotment.

—like the other organic laws—never submitted to Parliament at all. It was restrictive, requiring a single package vote on all 'continuing services' (*services votés*) which absorb about six-sevenths of the budget; parliamentary control was thereby impeded though (contrary to a widely-held view) it was not ruled out. The new rules allowed civil servants and ministers to draw up their proposals in much less rushed and frantic conditions than in the past, and they sharply reduced the time taken on the budget in the Assembly.[3]

There was a price to be paid. According to an academic authority who is also a former senator and a Gaullist politician, the organization of the budget debates 'since 1959 seems to be dominated by a single objective: speed. This horror of losing time consumes the managers of the National Assembly, the rapporteurs-généraux and the government'.[4] Members were short of time and staff to supervise the administration effectively.[5] Sitting nine or ten hours daily (except Sundays) for three weeks, they could still allow only four hours on the estimates for the ministry of labour and social security.[6] Under pressure from the government, if one estimate was dealt with more quickly than expected, another was rushed in to fill the time—so that when the estimates for the overseas departments were debated, most of their deputies were absent and so was their minister.[7] At first members could talk at reasonable length, but in the later stages the President might restrict them to a minute or ninety seconds only.[8] To all these grievances the UNR spokesmen had their standard reply: Michel Debré had convinced himself that the House of Commons votes the budget in a single afternoon and this extraordinary error was repeated time and again by official apologists.[9] But they also made some attempt to meet the complaints. In the worst years, 1959 and

---

[3] From 383 hours in 1950 to only 100 ten years later—though it crept up again to 143 in 1963 and 144 in 1966 (plus supplementaries). It had less time under the 1956 procedure.

[4] Léo Hamon and C. Emeri in *RDP* 80.1 (Jan. 1964), pp. 8off. (quotation, p. 81).

[5] Pierre Bas (UNR), quoted *ibid.*, p. 85; Chandernagor, *op. cit.*, pp. 132-3. But the finance committee has civil servants seconded to it, whose services are not always fully used.

[6] *Ibid.*, p. 81; cf. P. Viansson-Ponté in *Monde*, 22 Oct. 1964. The chairman of the finance committee, J. P. Palewski, thought the total time allowed Parliament by the constitution was five days too short: *JO* 9 Nov. 1963, p. 7114. However, some brief floor debates were on subjects which had been examined very thoroughly in committees or study groups.

[7] Hamon and Emeri, *loc. cit.*, pp. 81-2.

[8] *Ibid.*, quoting *JO* 5 Nov. 1963, p. 6481. But his rigour varied with the subject, and a serious speaker on an important issue could always have adequate time.

[9] *JO* (*Sénat*) 21 Dec. 1959, p. 1923, cf. *JO* 10 Nov. 1966, p. 4537; Y. Guéna in *Monde*, 10 Dec. 1963.

1963, the administration had been at fault in laying its bills late in the day; the respective prime ministers admitted this and promised to—and did—do better next year; the constitutional amendment of 1963 eased the situation somewhat by extending the autumn session from seventy-four to eighty days.

Another complaint, heard not only on the budget, was that far too much of the limited time was taken up by the majority. On the education estimates of 1963 Gaullist ministers, Gaullist rapporteurs and Gaullist party spokesmen took seven hours, leaving the various opposition parties only two and a half hours to put their different viewpoints—though it is true that the Gaullist rapporteurs were very often extremely critical of the government they theoretically supported.[10] Complaints about the pressure of time are more often heard in public than in private, for it is electioneering speeches rather than serious criticism which suffers most from it. The budget is still, therefore, much the most useful occasion for questioning and scrutinizing the government's policies. It is far better than ordinary question-time because debate is less restricted by the rules, the minister has to attend at a known time, and above all a vote can be taken. Consequently the same members often raise on the budget points which they had previously brought up in question-time without getting satisfaction.[11] Indeed the government itself often refuses statements of policy in the autumn session and urges its critics to raise their complaints on the budget.[12]

On the whole, then, the budgetary procedure of the Fifth Republic was a great improvement. The government could be sure of getting its business without undue delay. The budget is now regularly voted before Christmas, a feat never achieved in the previous thirty years, and in 1964 the minister proudly presented to the television audience (given precedence over Parliament) what he claimed was the first balanced budget for thirty years.[13] With its mastery of procedure and its loyal majority the cabinet could carry its proposals without serious alteration and sometimes even without a major political battle, as in 1960 and 1966. In 1961, 1963 and 1964 it succeeded at the price of some concessions to senatorial opposition and pressure from the conference committee; and even when controversy was sharper, as in 1959, 1962 and 1965, it was able to insist on inserting its own amendments

[10]Hamon and Emeri, loc. cit., p. 83; Avril, Régime (2nd ed.), p. 387. Guéna, loc. cit., agreed that more of the available time should be allotted to the opposition.

[11]Ameller, pp. 191–2.

[12]Hamon and Emeri, loc. cit., p. 87. Cf. P. Avril in RDP 81.3 (May 1965), p. 455n.; Pierre Dumas, JO 2 Oct. 1965, p. 3278.

[13]For the way it was 'balanced' see Marcel Pellenc's speech (below, p. 81n.).

into the conference committee's draft and carrying them in a package vote.[14] In effect, therefore, the conference committee procedure lets the government, on the budget as elsewhere, impose its wishes frequently on the Senate and occasionally on both houses.[15]

Thus in the last resort power rests with the government. Nevertheless Parliament can exercise more influence than the constitution might suggest. In the first Parliament, each house passed about half the budgetary amendments put forward on the floor and two-thirds of those proposed by the rapporteur-general of the finance committee.[16] Since that National Assembly had a right-wing majority its influence was naturally exerted far more effectively in favour of industry and commerce than of the working class, whose political friends were in opposition. But even the Communists managed to win acceptance for 28 per cent of their amendments, the UNR for half theirs, and the Conservatives—the party of successive ministers of finance—for 60 per cent. In the second Assembly a stronger left-wing opposition showed that it was not unwilling to act on behalf of business and peasant pressure-groups, notably in the TVA debate of December 1965 when it had the majority on the run.[17] But as a rule the government's supporters displayed much better discipline in the second Parliament than in the first, and it was rare for ministers to change their minds under pressure exerted in public.[18]

It by no means followed that Parliament's influence was weaker: only that it was exercised behind the scenes rather than on the stage. Opposition members who wanted to bring about a change of policy, rather than to organize a demonstration, knew that the government was often ready to make in committee concessions which it would refuse on the floor. Gaullist supporters could discuss their criticisms with the minister in private and induce him to change his mind;

[14]Only in 1959 did it have to call for a vote of confidence—on the perennially dangerous estimate for the ministry of ex-servicemen. The 1962 package vote enabled it to insist on reversing the Assembly's previous vote in favour of a four-year plan for ex-servicemen, and on making the contributors to the general social security system pay for higher benefits in the agricultural sector.

[15]P. Delvolvé and H. Lesguillons, *Le Contrôle parlementaire sur la politique économique et budgétaire* (Paris 1964).

[16]Half the successful amendments were put forward in his name—some being his own, some moved on behalf of the committee. On amendments in the first Parliament see P. Lalumière in *Monde*, 27–28 Oct. 1963.

[17]Below, p. 94.

[18]In 5 years Parliament had altered the budget only 0.01 or 0.001%: Henri Duffaut (Soc.), *JO* 10 Nov. 1966, p. 4534. In 1966—an election year—the ministry of defence proposed to curtail severely cheap fare concessions for soldiers going on leave, then gave way to vigorous protests from majority and opposition alike. But some cynics suspected that this unpopular proposal was put forward as a 'lightning-conductor' to attract parliamentary attention away from more serious matters.

occasionally a rapporteur with a strong case and some sympathy within the government, like Jean Royer over housing in 1966, could lead a successful revolt. Much more often his criticisms, seemingly unheeded in one year, would bear fruit on the following budget. But the channels of influence were limited, for effective pressure behind the scenes could normally be exerted only by influential Gaullists or by finance committee members, above all the rapporteurs.[19] Pressure-groups—and spending ministries—therefore sought to influence the minister of finance by feeding their information and proposals to a member of the committee and lobbying for them among his colleagues. A public battle on the floor of the house was often a sign of weakness rather than of strength.[20]

The new situation enabled the government to predict with much more confidence the reaction of Parliament to its proposals. The budget could be prepared in more orderly conditions, and the departments no longer had to rely for their appropriations on provisional twelfths spread over half the year. These changes greatly improved administration; they could also have made possible a genuine parliamentary scrutiny over the working of government which the traditional budgetary disorder had seriously impeded. But the administration resorted to a variety of expedients to nullify any effective parliamentary check. The procedure of 1956 had required the finance committee's approval for transfers of credits; the new rules did not, and the government has often taken improper advantage of its freedom, making transfers of amounts bigger than the original estimate, or between ministries, or even to pay for altogether new purposes. It often brings in large supplementaries, which misuse authority given for increasing expediture on certain limited items to allow it to pay for objects not originally intended. And sometimes it postpones to a later year expenditure already authorized; while this practice may have good economic justification, Parliament is frustrated when the amounts involved, together with those of the supplementary estimates, may (as in 1960 and 1961) reach a total larger than that of all the new authorizations on which alone it is allowed to pronounce. With so many devices enabling the government to dispose of 'free money', parliamentary control is easily evaded.[21]

[19]Majority members of the committee naturally had more influence than their opposition colleagues. But many of the latter were less assiduous, and therefore less effective than they might have been.

[20]I am greatly indebted to Mr. Guy Lord's unpublished work on the French budgetary process throughout this chapter, and particularly here.

[21]Lesguillons, op. cit., pp. 208–13, 215, 219, 220n, 224; annual reports of the Cour des Comptes, cited e.g. by Marcel Pellenc, JO (Sénat), 4 July 1963, pp. 1490–2. For recent complaints by the two rapporteurs-généraux see Louis Vallon's report, Monde 29 Nov. 1966, and speeches, JO 24 Nov. 1966, pp. 4840–1, 1 Dec. 1966, pp. 5126–7; Marcel Pellenc's report, Monde 13 Dec. 1966,

Moreover, the government further abuses its advantages and diminishes the limited time which Parliament enjoys by tacking to the budget measures which have nothing to do with finance. In the past it was private members who proposed such 'riders'; now ministers have discovered their advantages—quicker passage, and perhaps a way to by-pass a tiresome committee. Thus the 1964 supplementaries included proposals to set up a new forests authority, authorize increased rents, override certain legal decisions by the *Conseil d'Etat,* and even rectify errors in bills for which the government had insisted on a package vote. Half the clauses fell outside the nominal object of the bill, and of the time spent on it in the Assembly only one-fifteenth was devoted to finance; the rapporteur-general of the Senate's finance committee, Marcel Pellenc, complained he had 'never seen such a monument of anomalies, irregularities and illegalities.'[22] Once again the government finds itself so thoroughly protected against the abuses of the past that it has felt strong enough to commit new abuses of its own, and may bring into discredit a progressive reform.

(II) THE ROLE OF THE PRIVATE MEMBER

Perhaps the most spectacular of all the financial changes is contained in Article 40 of the constitution, which forbids private members' proposals to increase public expenditure or reduce revenue. Based on British practice and meeting an old Conservative demand, this ban was only the culmination of a long process which by 1958 was (except to Communists) almost uncontroversial. For, during the Fourth Republic, this right of the deputies had been so severely limited that, even before the regime fell, they were willing to abandon it altogether. Article 40 merely included in the new constitution restraints which had hitherto depended on an ordinary law.[23] At first it was applied with a rigidity which irritated members, who had accepted similar restrictions in the past but now resented the way they were operated— and the absence of other outlets for their own frustration. In 1961 a Gaullist deputy, interested in getting higher pensions for ex-servicemen on the railways, proposed to reduce the estimates for the ministry

and speech, *JO (Sénat),* 13 Dec. 1966, pp. 2406–11; cf. complaints about the road fund, *ibid.* 20 Nov. 1966, pp. 2147–54. Mitterrand's shadow cabinet accused the government of cancelling expenditure, already voted by Parliament, three days after the house had risen, by a decree which was not to be published in the *JO* (this was done by Giscard, and revealed by Debré). See *Monde,* 7 and 22–23 May 1966.

[22]*JO (Sénat)* 14 Dec. 1964, p. 2293. For later complaints by Gaullists see *JO* 1 Dec. 1966, pp. 5127–8, 5138–9 (MM. de Grailly for the legislation committee, Le Theule for the defence committee, Krieg); cf. pp. 5130–1, M. de Tinguy (MRP): 'it's not just a rider, it's the whole horse guards'.

[23]*CCC,* p. 114 (statement by the government's spokesman).

F

of transport in order to make up the cost; standing orders were successfully invoked against him—and the estimates were rejected by a large
majority.[24] During the first Parliament only sixteen private members'
bills on fiscal matters were introduced and none of them passed,
though amendments to proposed new taxes were frequently successful.[25] But in the old days restrictions had been applied strictly only
during the budget debates (when the danger of log-rolling amendments was greatest) and that old convention soon revived, so that
the new rules were often applied more flexibly to ordinary bills than to
budgetary amendments.

There was a striking example in 1964, on the bill to consolidate the
pensions code. When the Assembly began its sitting there were 100
amendments proposed; when it finished, it had examined twice as
many and most of them were for higher expenditure. Both to save
money and to protect the simplifying provisions of the new code, the
minister frequently invoked Article 40—against UNR as well as
opposition members, and also against the committee on cultural and
social affairs. But sometimes he refrained—almost all the eighteen
amendments he accepted cost money—and sometimes he was frustrated, for the finance committee chairman had to confirm that Article
40 applied to a given proposal and he was not always willing to do
so.[26] The house finally voted the bill by 475 to 0 and sent it to the
Senate, which carried a flood of amendments (many of them infringing
Article 40) and voted the bill unanimously. When the deputies came
to consider the bill again their appetites had been whetted, and the
social affairs and defence committees brought forward many more
amendments including the senatorial ones. The government at first
tried conciliation, accepting eight amendments out of sixty, but then
called a halt and demanded a package vote in spite of bitter protests.
No one would oppose a bill improving pensions, but a third of those
who had previously supported it now abstained: it passed by only
320 to 0 on the second round, with 149 deputies abstaining, and by 197
to 0 in the 300-strong Senate.

(III) THE NEW SITUATION

The financial changes made in the Fifth Republic leave to Parliament
a budgetary role not unlike that of the House of Commons. More

[24]*JO* 7 Nov. 1961, pp. 3946–8; *Monde,* 9 Nov. 1961.
[25]Lalumière, *loc. cit.*
[26]There was some discrimination between the parties. Opposition members
tried three times to hold the government to its promise of 1962 to bring forward
a four-year plan for dealing with ex-servicemen's pensions; the minister tried to
refuse under Article 40; the finance committee asked for time to consider
whether it applied—and, after a UNR member had added his name to the
amendment, decided that it did not.

effective leadership and a better-controlled timetable are advantages which more than compensate for the private member's lost opportunities for constructive proposals—or for demagogic mischief-making. Discussions are sometimes excessively rushed, but even this is preferable to the inordinate delays which were liable to stultify whole sessions in the old days. But French deputies have not turned into Englishmen, and neither the members nor their constituents have abandoned the habits of the past. Parliamentary pressure still concentrates heavily, especially in an election year, on remedying the grievances of the traditional groups—farmers, soldiers, ex-servicemen—by bargaining with the government for small extra sums and finding procedural devices for evading the new restrictions in order to make the pressure effective. Except for the few rapporteurs who are at once able, influential and assiduous, the members of the majority exert little influence on major policy; and members of the opposition carry so little weight that few of them even try.

This is not primarily a responsibility of the Gaullist regime. In France as elsewhere the annual budget has lost both its dominance over the legislative year and its decisive importance for policy-making. It remains the crucial instrument for investigating and criticizing the way the government uses its powers and executes in practice such long-term measures as the bill for a nuclear deterrent force, or the national Plan (which Parliament debates far more fully in the Fifth Republic than in the Fourth). But the freedom of both members and ministers to use the annual budget to alter policy is severely limited by their past approval for these long-term measures. The budget as a policy-making instrument therefore matters far less today than in past regimes. This decline is essentially a response to long-term changes which are equally evident in other countries and other aspects of legislative influence. But the change has been accentuated by the working of the new regime.

VI

Five Legislative
Case Studies

This chapter traces the parliamentary progress of five bills: one delegating to the government power to legislate against alcoholism and other 'social scourges'; one financial measure extending the scope of the value-added tax (TVA); a reform of the law of adoption; a fairly mild proposal concerning the right to strike; and a major reorganization of the State broadcasting and television service, ORTF.

Political attitudes to these measures were very different. On the last two there was a party clash which broadly pitted the majority against the opposition. Adoption was a topic arousing strong emotional feelings, but this bill—like many others in 1965–66—provoked no conflict between parties; a startling fact pointing to a great change in the attitude of the Communists, who had hitherto opposed every measure of any importance in order to emphasize their total hostility to the existing political and social order. On alcoholism and the TVA, the government came under converging pressure from parliamentarians, particularly senators, of all parties on behalf of small business and the peasantry. Nor was it only Socialist and Communist politicians who sought to extend their normal clientele; on the strike bill the Republican Independents (Conservative Gaullists) took up the defence of the trade unions—and the government was well aware that their open discontent was usually a sign of covert dissatisfaction within the well-disciplined ranks of the UNR. But even those ranks were shattered, like those of British Conservatives over resale price maintenance in 1964, when they were subjected to really heavy constituency pressure in an election year.

The working of the new legislative procedure is also illustrated by these five bills. It was only because the Constitutional Council gave a broad interpretation to the scope of legislation under Article 34 that the most far-reaching of them, that on the ORTF, was sent to Parliament at all. The old committee spirit emerged over alcoholism, where it was a standing committee that led the critics; the government's new advantages were shown on the strike bill, where it was beaten in committee owing to the slackness of its supporters but easily retrieved the situation on the floor. The package vote was frequently indispensable to keep the majority in line, but over the ORTF it irritated into outright hostility critics who were eager to achieve a reasonable compromise. The Senate was a centre of opposition on all four controversial bills. Two of these went to conference committee: on the strike bill it brought no agreed solution but enabled the hesitant majority members to signify their discontent and win concessions; on the ORTF it first operated with remarkable success to achieve a compromise on a highly political measure, but was later manipulated by the government to impose its own views. On the TVA, a financial bill where the executive seemed well guarded against parliamentary pressure, the constitutional and political barriers could be seen collapsing as electoral panic eroded the loyalty of the majority. The same would certainly have happened if an ordinary bill had sought to check alcoholism; instead, therefore, this was the single case in the first two Parliaments when the government sought delegated legislative powers under Article 38 on an ordinary domestic matter. Even so, much scope remains for a really determined opposition to exploit old-style procedural manoeuvres, and the proposals survived only because the government flagrantly violated the spirit of the constitution—for which it later had to pay when it wanted to use Article 38 for more acceptable purposes.

(1) THE 'SOCIAL SCOURGES' BILL, 1960

The privilege of the *bouilleurs de cru,* which allows owners of fruit trees to distil a small quantity of tax-free alcohol for their private use, was widely extended in the twentieth century. Their numbers swelled from a few thousand to over three million; the alcohol they distilled found its way in large quantities to the black market; chronic alcoholism grew more prevalent in France than in any other major country, especially in the regions where the *bouilleurs* were most numerous; and they developed into a highly-organized and truculent pressure-group with, so politicians believed, an unusually large number of followers willing to vote against any candidate who threatened their privilege. Only one government of the Fourth Republic attempted to tackle this notorious scandal. In 1954 Mendès-France used his special legislative powers to strike at alcoholism in its various forms, and confined the *bouilleurs'* privilege to *bona fide* farmers—thus excluding not only fringe beneficiaries like the 10,000 *bouilleurs* of Paris, but also the travelling distillers who were the main agents of political agitation, the main channel to the black market, and the main threat to the treasury. But he soon fell from power (partly as a result) and under his successor, Edgar Faure, the Assembly voted by more than two to one to postpone the application of the decree for a year, Mendesists from rural areas (notably François Mitterrand) voting in the majority along with the parties of the Left. Each year thereafter the decree was 'postponed' again.

The few politicians who felt strongly on the subject included most women deputies, some MRP members, Mendès-France and Michel Debré, whose father, a distinguished doctor, was active in the campaign against alcoholism. In September 1958 Debré's journal cited Parliament's conduct towards the *bouilleurs* as striking evidence of the political cowardice of Fourth Republican politicians; the very next day the government in which he sat postponed the decree for yet another year so as not to lose *bouilleurs'* votes at the coming referendum. But four months later Debré became prime minister and he promptly tackled the problem, introducing at the end of 1959 a bill which preserved the privilege for existing *bouilleurs* but denied them the right to transfer it to their children. It was symptomatic of his changing attitude to special committees of the Assembly that the premier now refused to set one up, despite protests from the pressure-group, and sent the bill to an ordinary standing committee instead.[1] When it came before the house in December, the *bouilleurs'* secretary, a former Conservative deputy, sat in the public gallery instructing his agents on the floor just as Pierre Poujade had done four years before— at a sitting often quoted by Gaullists to illustrate the peculiar decadence of the Fourth Republic. The Assembly mangled the bill and the Senate gave it short shrift, rejecting it by 110 to 55.

For his second attempt Debré chose a circuitous route. In July 1960 he brought in under Article 38 a bill giving the government temporary legislative powers to act against various 'social scourges': alcoholism, prostitution, cancer, tuberculosis and heart-disease. He hoped that members of Parliament would accept the measure more readily when they did not have to take personal responsibility for the government's decisions—a classic reason for special powers legislation in the past. But the committee on social affairs was not deceived and voted the previous question, which is equivalent to rejection without debate. The rapporteur was a UNR woman deputy; she resigned her post, and Debré brought the bill to the house without a committee report (he could not have done so in past regimes). He warned members that if it was rejected he would allow the Mendès-France decree to go into force; the *bouilleurs* could thus be struck at merely through the government doing nothing. This was Debré's only trump card, and the deputies' best excuse for appeasing their wrathful constituents. Fearing the Mendès-France decree and for no other reason, the Assembly rejected a motion for the previous question, though only two deputies spoke for the bill. Then the government decided to

[1] On this point see above, pp. 62, 64.

drop the medical scourges, a new draft emerged from committee, homosexuality was added on a snap amendment from the floor; and the deputies sent the bill on to the Senate. The senators were again warned, by both the premier and the minister of health, that if the bill failed the Mendès-France decree would be enforced; and by a brilliant piece of counter-lobbying a UNR deputy, Louis Briot, who was national chairman of the *bouilleurs'* parliamentary committee, was persuaded to write a letter saying that the bill was the lesser evil—though his organization in the country thought it the greater. Under this pressure it passed the Senate by 161 to 93, and the Assembly on second reading by 323 to 131, conferring on the government powers for four months to make ordinances having the force of law. These would lapse unless laid before Parliament for ratification by December 15. A day before the time-limit expired and two days before the end of the session, the ordinances were duly laid—but were not called for debate.[2] The government business for the day was a proposed constitutional amendment changing the dates of parliamentary sessions; but Briot in true Fourth Republican style moved the previous question and so forced a debate on alcoholism instead. He was appeased by a government promise not to put the measures into effect until Parliament met again four months later. By that time another referendum would be safely past.

The crisis came in the following session. The ratification bill had been duly laid and, whether or not it was debated, the ordinances could now go into force. In May the social affairs committee, through a UNR doctor deputy, reported favourably on all but two ordinances—but the government still refused to put the bill on the agenda, fearing the wrecking amendments which the *bouilleurs'* friends would certainly move. The Presidents' Conference put it down for three days when there was no government business, but the government at once introduced enough business of its own, which took priority, to fill up all three sittings. The committee chairman (a rural UNR member) agreed to postpone the bill on the understanding that this was not just a delaying tactic; a month later he realized that it was, and protested that the government was misusing its right to priority despite its repeated promises to allow Parliament to discuss the bill. Another month passed; the ordinances were still in force and the session was due to end in ten days. For July 18 the government had put down a bill setting up the Paris District, a new regional authority; a Conservative member from Normandy, a *bouilleurs'* stronghold, moved the previous question. The minister of finance warned that this would only kill the District bill without helping the ratification bill. He

[2]They provoked a protest demonstration outside the Assembly by the Paris prostitutes—accompanied, in an unwonted gesture of solidarity, by the homosexuals.

told the house that the prime minister had already met the chairmen of all the parliamentary parties in an effort at compromise, and promised to see them again in October and, if they agreed on amendments which the government could accept, to bring up the amended bill then for ratification. But the credibility gap had widened, and the Assembly voted the previous question. (Luckily for the government, the Senate had accepted the District bill; for once, therefore, the senators were supporting the government against the deputies, as had originally been expected, and it was able to use the conference committee to revive its bill, which then duly passed.)

The ratification was not put on the agenda in October. Now the Assembly's discontent reached a new peak. The production committee voted unanimously—in sharp contrast to the social affairs committee a few months before—against ratifying any of the ordinances. At this point the government brought in a new bill seeking delegated powers under Article 38;[3] although its purpose was uncontroversial (to help resettle refugees from North Africa), the Assembly rejected it by a majority of two because of ministers' behaviour over the *bouilleurs'* affair. The government called for a second deliberation and this time, though the legislation committee again opposed the new bill, the Assembly voted it by a large majority. But the deputies demonstrated their continuing suspicion by limiting the period within which the government could act to five months instead of twelve, and requiring the ratification bill to be laid by June.

A year later there was a new National Assembly, in which the UNR had an assured majority. From time to time Briot still tried to have the *bouilleurs'* ratification bill on the agenda; but the main effort came from another quarter in the autumn of 1964. The Socialist opposition, combining a defence of democratic principle with an appeal for *bouilleurs'* votes, protested that the government was suppressing the ratification bill. Virtuously and forgetfully, the minister replied that the government had never opposed discussion of it, and that the Presidents' Conference could put it on the supplementary agenda at any time. When told 'your majority stops us', he blandly answered 'That's democracy'. The Socialist spokesmen then challenged the minister to debate the Socialists' proposed constitutional amendment (introduced three years earlier and never discussed) to provide that ordinances made under Article 38 laws should lapse unless the ratification bill were voted on within six months. The minister retorted that his opponent 'simply wants the minority to decide the parliamentary timetable. I know of no democracy in the world which allows that.'[4] Blocked in the Assembly, the *bouilleurs* still found a last line

[3]See above, p. 73.
[4]*JO* 17 Nov. 1964, pp. 5416–7. The minister, Jean Foyer, had been a professor of public law!

of defence in the Senate, which wrote into the budget for 1965 a clause requiring the ratification bill to be brought up for debate by May 1, 1965. The deputies rejected it and so, after the ordinances had been in force for nearly four years without ever being approved by Parliament, the parliamentary struggle to abrogate them at last petered out.

Mainly because of Debré's personal commitment, the Fifth Republic had successfully lanced an abscess which had long poisoned the life of the Third and Fourth. This was not because the politicians of those regimes were uniquely cowardly, as Debré had once argued. For his own followers themselves would accept his policy only if they were protected against the consequences, first by an abdication of parliamentary responsibility as inglorious as any in the past, and later by the government's totally unscrupulous misuse of the facilities the constitution gave it. Nevertheless, the opposition might have launched its protest on behalf of parliamentary liberties from less insalubrious terrain.

(2) THE STRIKES (EARLY WARNING) BILL, 1963

In January 1962 Michel Debré, with his usual restless anxiety to settle problems, had proposed to the cabinet a rather stringent strike bill requiring a four to six weeks cooling-off period, a committee of inquiry, and a ballot among the workers at the start and end of a strike. It appears that President de Gaulle stopped the discussion after this bill met strong opposition from two ministers of progressive views, Robert Buron and Pierre Sudreau.[5] Three months later Debré was out of power, and a year after that his successors so mishandled the great miners' strike that they provoked a wave of almost universal public sympathy—headed by the bishops and even sweeping *Le Figaro* with it—which brought the miners a very favourable settlement and lowered the President's prestige to its nadir. Perhaps this success encouraged illusions among the unions, for they soon began a series of lightning protest strikes on the Paris public transport system. By calling out one group of men after another for a few hours at a time without warning, they effectively disrupted the system—and utterly exasperated the public, particularly the poor who depend on buses and the Metro to commute between Paris and the suburbs.

Seizing its opportunity, the government brought in early in July 1963 a bill to regulate strikes in the public service. These were to be

[5]Buron, a left-wing MRP leader, resigned with his party in May over European policy. Sudreau, a strong-minded ex-prefect, was to resign in September in protest against the unconstitutional method used to amend the constitution.

preceded by five days' notice (often voluntarily given already); could be called only by 'representative' unions (widely interpreted); would entail losing at least a day's pay however short the strike; and could not be pursued by calling out different groups in succession. The Assembly's social affairs committee chose a UNR rapporteur by forty-two to fourteen for a Socialist. It sat with the legislation committee to hear the prime minister put his case; but it voted against hearing spokesmen for the unions by thirty-six to seventeen with five abstainers, three of them UNR. At the first vote many government supporters were absent and an alternative draft, presented by MRP and stressing conciliation instead of sanctions, was carried instead of the goverment's bill. In the old days this would have been the version discussed on the floor; now, however, the government's bill came before the house anyway.

When the bill came to the Assembly the Socialists at once moved the previous question, but lost 315 to 146 because MRP hoped to bring forward its own proposals as amendments. But the government warned that it would accept no obligation to negotiate or seek arbitration, and would call for a package vote against any important amendments; MRP therefore turned against the bill, which was carried only by 257 to 205. In the Senate the social affairs committee chose a Socialist rapporteur, who told the house that his committee saw no point in amending the bill since it knew that ministers meant to demand a package vote; when they did so, the Conservative senators—like the MRP deputies—swung round from opposing the previous question (rejected 145–78) to opposing the bill itself (rejected 203–35). The bill went to conference committee which split equally, 7–7, on both the government bill and the MRP draft: as a tie is negative in French procedure, both were rejected. A compromise was then put forward striking out everything after Clause 1 (which stated to whom the bill would apply), and affirming that the government would lay a new bill in six months' time after discussion with the unions. The seven senators voted for it, the six UNR deputies opposed it—and the one RI deputy abstained, so that this proposal became the report of the conference committee. When the government took the bill back to the Assembly, it insisted on its original draft, but recognized the dissatisfaction of the RIs by promising that the unions would in fact be consulted—while saving face by refusing to specify this in the bill. The Assembly then passed the measure by the same majority as before (257–204) and after another rejection in the Senate (213–35) the deputies voted it into law by show of hands only three weeks after the cabinet had first adopted it.

The unions were not crippled, but the lightning strikes ended—either on account of the bill, or of their unpopularity which had made its passage possible. But their lobbying had no effect at all.

The transport strikes had forfeited the sympathy which the miners' strike had won them, and there was no sign of any public response to their violent agitation against the bill. The government made its minor concessions to the RIs, whose open irritation signified as usual some concealed resentment in the UNR. The political friends of the unions were in opposition and could do less for them than a marginal majority group which perhaps had less sympathy for them than any other party, but always liked to demonstrate its independent attitude and concern for the rights of Parliament.

(3) THE BROADCASTING BILL, 1964[6]

No subject could be more politically contentious than that of government control of broadcasting. Always used and abused by the ministers in power (notably the Socialists in 1956), it was the subject of sixteen bills in the Fourth Republic—not one of them debated, let alone passed. When the Gaullists came to power they dominated broadcasting more thoroughly than any of their predecessors, partly because they stayed longer in office and therefore had more chance to instal their own men, partly because the President of the Republic considered television as his main weapon for combating the nefarious criticisms of the press. But the demand grew to put the organization of broadcasting on a proper legal footing, and the government decided to accede to it. They wanted to act by regulations rather than a bill. This preference was not to avoid either a debate, which they promised in any event, or even a vote on detailed amendments, for they could rely on their majority not to accept the 'BBC status' which the opposition proposed; it was apparently to preserve flexibility in changing the organization in the light of experience. But when ministers referred the matter to the Constitutional Council, that supposedly ultra-Gaullist body, applying its usual criteria, laid down that five of the seven main parts of the proposed measure fell within the domain of the law. The government then decided to bring the whole subject before Parliament —including the parts where the Council would have allowed it to act on its own.

The bill was a short one of only nine clauses, making arrangements on broad lines rather than in detail. The first reading debate was held at the end of May 1964 both on it and on three private members' bills from the opposition; a very full one, it took up three parliamentary days. The house was given a very free rein and allowed to vote amendments on quite detailed points, regulating the method of choosing the deputies' representatives on the Broadcasting Advisory Council

---

[6]For a fuller account see M. Bouissou in *RDP* 80.6 (Nov. 1964), pp. 1109–97.

and its supervision of the Assembly's own debates.[7] But the government refused two of the major amendments, one on the composition
of the Administrative Council and one requiring a minimum number
of party political broadcasts. In a second deliberation of a few minutes
only, it obliged the deputies to vote these down in a package vote,
taken on the redrafted measure without the two offending clauses.
It was thus the government bill, substantially intact, which went to
the Senate. There, in another full debate, the bill was transformed
by amendments into the form desired by the opposition. A conference
committee was called and, though each house chose its conferees only
from its own majority, they reached agreement on this highly controversial measure by eleven votes to none—with three abstentions, said
to be two UNR deputies and a Communist senator. The basis of
the compromise was that the upper house abandoned most of its
amendments, notably those strengthening the Administrative Council
and buttressing its independence, in return for a legally guaranteed
right of reply to criticism in a broadcast or television performance.
The government, however, refused the compromise (allegedly because
the minister, who had agreed to it unofficially, was overruled by the
Elysée). In the Assembly a conference report can be amended only
with the government's consent; the minister brought in this one with
amendments imposed by him to cancel all the concessions made to
the opposition. The majority followed their instructions and voted
the bill in this form, against senatorial opposition, on June 25.

Here, therefore, was a situation not unlike that in Britain when a
government of the Left enters into conflict with the Lords. The
ministry with the support of a majority in the lower house can
readily override the upper; the discussion may be long and ample
but in the end the cabinet will get its way, allowing parliamentary
amendments on minor points but not on major ones. Yet it would
be wrong to assume that the final outcome would have been the same
if the broadcasting measure had been brought into force by regulations
in the first place, as the government had once wished. The minister
would have drafted his measure differently—and no doubt more restric-
tively—if he had had to face no parliamentary scrutiny. Moreover,
in the debates he gave assurances about the government's future use
of its powers, and his statements could be quoted later as evidence of
the intentions of the legislator: the administrative courts can thus
apply, in cases arising out of regulations made under the act, criteria
which are available only because Parliament had its say. The political

[7]The government could have had these amendments ruled out by appealing to
the Constitutional Council; and with its consent would still be entitled under
Article 37 to alter these arrangements by regulation later. (Earlier, arguing
against submitting the bill to Parliament, the minister had perversely—and
erroneously—denied that he could do so: *JO* 14 June 1963, pp. 3416-9, cf.
Bouissou, *loc. cit.*, p. 1122; contrast Pompidou, *JO* 18 May 1967, p. 1067.)

consequences were also instructive. In the 1965 presidential election the opposition candidates were allowed ample opportunity on television over a two-week campaign, and made an immense impact even in this short time because of the novelty of serious criticism on a screen hitherto reserved exclusively for persons acceptable to the authorities.[8] The conciliatory attitude of the UNR deputies had been shrewder, as well as more liberal, than the rigid determination of the executive to exploit its powers to the full. The lesson was learned, and though the television news programmes were no model of objectivity in 1966, the opposition had more opportunities to express its views in feature programmes than ever before in the Fifth Republic.

(4) THE VALUE-ADDED TAX, 1965

The value-added tax was almost universally approved by responsible extra-parliamentary opinion on both Left and Right. It already applied to industry, and the bill aimed at extending it to transport, distribution, most services and (with qualifications) to agriculture. This was required both under France's Common Market obligations and in her own interests, to compete with Germany who had already reformed her fiscal system and adopted the tax because of its progressive economic effects (it gave substantial encouragement to investment). It was also administratively useful, greatly simplifying the fiscal system and sweeping away many existing taxes on distribution. Chief of these was the local sales tax which had provoked the Poujadist movement in 1955, and was condemned for its inequitable incidence by everyone except the big-city mayors who benefited from it. The new tax was to raise only a sum equivalent to those it was superseding.

Debré's government twice brought in bills on the subject in 1959 and 1961, but he withdrew the first because of opposition and the second was buried in committee and never disinterred. Pompidou first proposed it in 1963, but postponed and modified it to meet objections (notably on local government finance) from the UNR's fiscal subject group.[9] In June 1965 it was brought forward in the Assembly, and an attempt to refer it back to committee was defeated. Of the 203 amendments put down, the government accepted 59, costing about £70,000,000. (One, exempting the press, was left to a free vote and carried by 459 to 3.) The house passed the bill easily, and the Socialists, Radicals and MRP, who abstained, said they would support it on its next reading if it were amended meanwhile. When it went to the Senate in October there were another 159 proposed amendments, many of them blatantly demagogic. The government warned that if too many people were exempted, a higher rate would

[8]This view is held most strongly by Gaullist observers.
[9]On these groups see below, pp. 106–7.

have to be imposed on the rest in order to raise the required sum; the senators continued cheerfully voting exemptions but protested bitterly when asked to vote a general rate 3 per cent higher than at first proposed. Several clauses were dropped but they finally voted the bill in order not to appear obstructive; and though the conference committee failed to agree, some of the difficulties were harmoniously settled there. Because the ordinary session had been cut short by the presidential election, the government decided to send the bill back to the Assembly in a special December session. There seemed no reason to expect a parliamentary crisis.

The Assembly met on December 21, two days after President de Gaulle's not very impressive re-election. The UNR deputies were appalled at his poor showing at the first ballot; the opposition, hitherto so moderate, exploited their embarrassment without inhibitions, and the pressure-groups reverted as if by magic to all the tactics and devices of the old regime. With suspicion spreading between ministers and their majority, deals in the lobbies, late-night sittings, and hasty visits by premier and finance minister to the UNR party meeting, the Palais Bourbon seemed to have reverted to the Fourth Republic in its worst days, when Pierre Poujade's political blackmail intimidated the Assembly before the eyes of the public.

The government made matters worse by allowing the house too little time. The rapporteur-general's report was distributed only twenty-five minutes before the Assembly met, and the finance committee did not help the government resist the flood of amendments which it had had no chance to consider. As soon as the debate opened, a UNR member moved successfully to suspend the sitting—purporting to speak for the finance committee, which had not been asked and indeed had not met. On reassembly, the Socialists moved to refer the bill back to committee and were beaten only by 247 to 208: twenty-two deputies of the majority failed to vote against them and four actually voted with them. The parliamentary defenders of the self-employed and the small shopkeepers then went into action, led by the Conservatives and the Communists.[10] Pleas were put forward for everyone from shoemakers and small-cinema owners to second-hand car dealers. Faced with panic in the ranks of their supporters, the government made concessions all along the line, sometimes accepting from a Gaullist an amendment they had just rejected from an opposition member. These concessions reduced the yield of the tax by a further £130 million, all of it cut from the previous total of indirect taxation (although private members are not supposed to be able to propose a reduction of government revenue). In the end the bill as amended

[10]One of whom lapsed into incoherence when he lost a page or two in the middle of the set speech which had been supplied to him.

excluded most farmers, exempted a quarter of the artisans and shop-keepers entirely and left at most a fifth of them fully liable, allowed some small businessmen so to operate it as surreptitiously to increase their profit margins—and postponed its application for a year, i.e. till after the next general election.

The government, having gone to and beyond the limit of reasonable conciliation, now demanded a package vote. Apart from the Communists, all the opposition parties had conditionally promised support six months before, and their conditions had been amply met. The government exploited their predicament by claiming that this vote would reveal who were the true Europeans. But Socialists, MRP and Radicals all voted against the bill, while the Gaullists, having somewhat protected their electoral rear, now loyally rallied to its support. It had had 260 supporters in June, and found only seven fewer in December. But, despite all the concessions, the abstainers dropped from 159 to 21, while the opponents rose from 47 to 197. The bill was sent to the Senate with a demand for an immediate debate; the senators objected, wanting it left till the next session in three months time, and spent the two hours allotted for the debate in complaining that the time was too short (as indeed it was). They rejected the bill, and the deputies then voted it into law despite them. It was an episode which did little credit to the majority and less still to the Fourth Republican parties; as a left-wing weekly put it, 'It is absurd for the Left Opposition so to behave that Pompidou's government seems ... [to enlightened opinion] ... the promoter of an indispensable reform already too long delayed and too thoroughly diluted'.[11]

(5) THE ADOPTION BILL, 1966

Many bills in the later stages of the second Parliament passed without opposition, Socialists and Communists often abstaining and sometimes voting in favour. This absence of contention was a sign that the Communist party was changing its strategy, or perhaps its character, for it had regarded nothing as uncontentious under previous regimes; and also that the government was promoting generally acceptable proposals.

Among these non-political subjects, adoption aroused particularly strong and widespread emotions. French law on the subject was primarily designed for persons who changed their legal identity to preserve a family name and succession rights, but it was also applied to children adopted for their own good by foster-parents. Out of date, obscure and contradictory, it led to many tragic conflicts in the courts when natural parents, after abandoning a child at birth, later claimed

[11]*Nouvel Observateur*, 29 Dec. 1965. See also *Monde*, 23, 24, 25 Dec. 1965; and J. P. Dussaife in *RFSP* 16.3 (June 1966), pp. 521–31.

it back from foster-parents who had given it the only home it had known. The bill, carefully drafted in the ministry of justice and discussed thoroughly in the legislation committee of the Assembly, went through the house in November 1965 on a unanimous vote, after only three and a half hours debate. The government's proposals made it easier for foster-parents to adopt children, provided they had no legitimate child of their own. The Left wanted to allow them to do so even then, subject to safeguards; the committee agreed; the minister opposed, fearing this easy way round the law on legitimizing illegitimate children; the committee's Left Gaullist chairman, René Capitant, spoke strongly for the amendment; and the Assembly voted it almost unanimously on a show of hands. But then the Senate came to the rescue of the Gaullist minister, and required parents with children of their own to obtain a dispensation from the President of the Republic —a solution to which the Assembly agreed. In the original bill the natural parent, having consented to an adoption, was allowed to withdraw consent within three months; a UNR member proposed to increase the period to six months; he was supported by a Communist and a Socialist but opposed by the minister and by the UNR rapporteur; and the amendment was lost. Another part of the bill dealt with foundlings, and with children abandoned by their parents to an institution. The parents had to be informed of the legal consequences and were entitled to withdraw their consent within three months; even afterwards, as long as the child was not with foster-parents, the prefect as its guardian could return it to the natural parents if he considered this in the child's interests. The Assembly strengthened the safeguards on their behalf, accepting both an RI amendment (they must be sent a model letter withdrawing consent, and told the address to which it should go) and a Communist one (they could appeal to a court against the prefect's refusal to return the child). The Senate voted several further amendments which the Assembly accepted without a conference committee being needed. Only twelve deputies were present for the final vote in June 1966. Once the bill went to the Senate, it took less than four weeks and only two readings in each house for an agreed version to pass into law with no opposition at any stage: a model of rapid and effective legislative cooperation.

These five bills show Parliament at work in various circumstances. The adoption bill is a case of effective cooperation on a matter arousing little political passion; the strike bill, of fairly straightforward political conflict; ORTF, of constructive compromise among the parliamentarians even in a party battle—though in the end the government successfully called on its followers to obey the whip. Three bills illustrate the impact of pressure-groups: weak and unpopular trade unions could gain only a little from a right-wing Assembly, but rural and small business groups can still count on widespread goodwill, especially in an election year. Even so, it is significant enough that Parliament could pass these acts at all—mostly by the normal procedure and all without a vote of confidence. For all five subjects had been under discussion for many years. A law on strikes was promised in the constitution of the Fourth Republic but never passed; alcoholism was the most notorious scandal of that regime; its Parliament discussed none of the sixteen bills proposed to regulate broadcasting; adoption and the TVA, though newer topics, were under debate well before 1958. The Fifth Republic could deal with them because the government could exercise effective leadership—and could therefore impose its own wishes if it chose, as it did over broadcasting and alcoholism. But it was conciliatory over the adoption bill, made some concessions over the strike measure—and abruptly discovered over the value-added tax that its procedural ramparts were vulnerable once its troops began to fear that loyalty was becoming a political liability. In that extreme case Gaullist politicians behaved very like their predecessors. But in more normal circumstances the new system allowed Parliament to legislate far more efficiently than the old.

VII

A Ministry
with a Majority

(I) THE FIRST PARLIAMENT

The new constitutional arrangements and the new political situation disconcerted parliamentarians of all parties. But the repercussions in the first Parliament were quite different from those in the second. The first was dominated by the immediate dangers arising from the Algerian crisis, which had led the politicians to bring de Gaulle to power and the people to approve the new regime. But this was thought of as a limited and exceptional period, which would end in due course and be followed by a return to 'politics as usual'. When the Gaullists unexpectedly returned stronger than ever in the second Parliament, these assumptions were shattered. Faced with the need to adapt to a new political structure which might last for a long time, and in which the government disposed of a secure majority and could not be upset by parliamentary manoeuvre, the politicians of the old order rarely succeeded in developing an effective opposition role. Instead they often withdrew into disgruntled absenteeism to plan lethargically for the distant election in which they could again hope at last to break the UNR's hold on the National Assembly.

When the first Parliament met in January 1959, it was dominated by the self-confident, aggressive and intransigent champions of all-out war in Algeria. At this time motions had not yet been declared unconstitutional, and the house soon showed its temper. In January it passed a UNR deputy's resolution in favour of integrating Algeria into France—a proposal which was clearly out of order, for it was moved after the special session had been closed.[1] In April René Pleven, a moderate leader from the Fourth Republic, tried to outdo the UNR in anti-Communist demagogy with a motion concerning an impending court case over the Polish library in Paris; although it plainly brought political pressure on the judiciary, it was carried by 467 to 10 against feeble government opposition. As a climax to this period of intolerance, Colonel Thomazo—a leading plotter of the May 13 crisis, who was shortly to resign from the UNR—tried to

[1]De Gaulle wrote a letter of rebuke to Chaban-Delmas for allowing it.

silence a young MRP deputy decorated while serving in Algeria, 'Private Lambert', whose views on the war displeased him. It was not surprising that the left-wing politicians, when they condemned the new rules which restricted their opportunities for criticizing the government, were warned by left-wing commentators like Maurice Duverger that any moves to revitalize the existing Parliament would only strengthen their most dangerous enemies and worsen de Gaulle's chance of settling the Algerian problem.

With the President's decision to opt for Algerian self-determination in September 1959, and the political and military rumblings which followed it, the parliamentary position was transformed. UNR deputies now had to choose between the leader to whom they owed allegiance—and their seats—and the cause which their most prominent spokesmen had upheld at the election. As they mostly followed de Gaulle, the old aggressive majority was broken. Henceforward a furiously resentful opposition on the Right, skilfully led by experienced parliamentarians like Georges Bidault, was challenging the new policies of a government which had abandoned the objectives both groups of men had originally supported. But the situation was complicated because the prime minister himself, while never refusing in the end to follow the President's line, still half clung to his former passionate convictions and constantly acted as a brake, always trying in practice to influence the new policies in the old direction. Partly as a result, de Gaulle found himself obliged to take the administration of Algerian policy out of the prime minister's hands and control it directly from the Elysée.

Another consequence was that those of the traditional parliamentary politicians who wanted a settlement of the conflict approved, instead of condemning, this supersession of the government which was responsible to Parliament by a President who was not. Their reasons were mixed. All were convinced that only de Gaulle could overcome military and settler resistance and bring the war to an end; all of them hoped he meant to do so, while none of them trusted Debré to move in the same direction. Some believed that since the dangerous men of the Right were so strong in the Assembly, it was their duty to support the President—if not the prime minister—in his difficult task. Others (or the same men) were privately convinced both that Algerian independence was inevitable and that it would ruin the statesman who conceded it: once de Gaulle had taken this burden on his shoulders and so discredited himself, they would bid to regain their lost power. Whatever their motives, therefore, the parliamentary leaders adopted 'submarine tactics', lying low while the war was on and waiting to surface when it ended. Parliament thus played little or no part in the great crises of the war, and this abdication naturally damaged its prestige.

Nor were the consequences confined to Algerian affairs. The domestic pressure-groups came—some of them rather slowly—to realize that

the direction of much of government policy was largely independent of
parliamentary influence, and they transferred their attention from the
once crowded lobbies, first to the corridors of ministries and then, if
they failed to get satisfaction, to the streets. For a time the principal
conflicts, domestic as well as external, seemed to by-pass Parliament
altogether. Members' morale sank to its lowest point. In July 1961 an
opposition deputy complained that the President's 'reserved domain'
(foreign, defence and Algerian affairs) was presumed to be too
important for Parliament, and the domain of regulations too trivial,
while its right to deal with anything in between was perpetually
contested. A UNR member the week before had put it more pithily:
'Perhaps we too should sit down in the Place de la Concorde to make
sure of a hearing'.[2]

Parliament was frustrated and impotent because the parties were
unable to express their real views. The new and bitter Algerian Right
was willing to use any tactical stratagem within the Assembly or any
illegal pressure from without to overthrow the ministry. But, as we
have seen, the traditional parties—Socialists, MRP, some Radicals
and even many Conservatives—were unwilling to defeat the government. Debré was thus protected not merely by the differences between
his opponents on Algerian and domestic issues, but also because even
where they could agree, on foreign and defence policy, the moderates
were unwilling to turn him out. Everyone knew that a majority of the
Assembly disliked the bill which authorized the French nuclear striking
force in the autumn of 1960, but it passed because the censure motions
against it attracted sixty fewer votes than were needed to carry
them.[3] The Algerian war, as Raymond Aron put it, served the government as a substitute for a majority—and so at first did the peace. In
June 1962 293 deputies, a comfortable majority of the total, signed a
declaration condemning the government's European policies; but they
neither pressed it to a vote of censure nor provided a majority for the
new censure motion on the nuclear striking force in the following
month.

The consequence was frustration all round, expressed in mass walk-
outs by the opposition deputies in September 1961 and June 1962.[4]
For the right-wing deputies, and all the senators, felt stultified by their
political impotence. So did the members of the Fourth Republican
parties, because of the constraints imposed on them by feelings of duty
or prudence. And so, not least, did the faithful UNR deputies, subjected to strains and temptations graver than those which ten years before
had shattered the last great Gaullist party, the RPF. Personal ambi-

[2]*JO* 11 and 18 July 1961, pp. 1576, 1748 (Louis Briot, UNR, and Patrice
Brocas, Radical).
[3]Above, pp. 55, 72.
[4]Above, pp. 44n., 52.

tions and electoral calculations had divided their ranks in 1952, and
the memory still rankled among Gaullist leaders, accounting in part
for their distrust of all parliamentarians, including their own followers.
But where the RPF had unexpectedly failed its creator, the UNR
proved loyal beyond anyone's predictions—even though its members
faced a far more uncomfortable situation. For, first, by supporting a
policy very different from the one on which many leading Gaullists had
campaigned in 1958, they exposed themselves to the taunts and invec-
tives of the unreconstructed *Algérie française* men—and perhaps
also, if public opinion resented the loss of Algeria, to an electoral tor-
pedo from the Fourth Republican 'submarine' politicians. Then the
UNR had to bear the brunt of any unpopular measures by Debré's
government. Its first budget, in December 1959, was framed by two
Conservative ministers—but carried in the Assembly by UNR votes,
only a quarter of the Conservatives supporting their own leaders
while rather more opposed them and the rest abstained.[5] At the same
time the Conservatives were vigorously exploiting the church schools
issue against the Gaullists just as the latter had done against the
Fourth Republican parties eight years earlier.

In spite of severe strains the UNR maintained the 'unconditional'
loyalty which traditionalists so despised and derided. Its solidarity was
the more creditable because neither the prime minister nor the President did much for the Gaullist rank and file. Debré had a rigid sense
of public service and administrative probity; he denied patronage to
his supporters, resisted party and pressure-group demands, and often
seemed to welcome his unpopularity as proof that he was doing his
duty without fear or favour. Consideration for his followers had never
been one of de Gaulle's preoccupations; the UNR deputies were
not consulted nor, apparently, were they respected. The President saw
no useful role for his lobby-fodder, and his natural detachment from
Parliament and party was accentuated by political circumstances which
required major policy to be controlled directly from the Elysée, by-
passing the prime minister responsible to Parliament. Finally, UNR
deputies recalled that at the last election the General had (vainly)
forbidden the use of his name 'even as an adjective'. They had no
guarantee that he would not do the same at the next.

With the end of the Algerian war matters began to improve. As the
risks of subversion and insurrection receded, political life settled back
into a normal—if drastically renovated—electoral and parliamentary
framework. With peace in Algeria and soon a Gaullist majority in the
Assembly, the President no longer had to fear that an active Parliament
would impede his freedom of action. The replacement of Debré also
helped, old parliamentarian though he was. For while in theory he
believed both in Parliament and in public criticism, in practice both

[5]Chapsal, *op. cit.*, p. 407.

soon made him impatient and angry. His successor was a less voracious worker and a less ardent reformer, not so tense a personality, and a much more conciliatory man. He did not have Debré's Jacobin contempt for pressure-groups, and he was not suspected of wanting to pursue a policy of his own, independent of de Gaulle's. The interests gradually realized that as the regime settled into a more regular routine, the Elysée no longer tried to short-circuit the ministries; and that as the government returned to normal, Parliament did so too. Their readjustment was somewhat delayed by the success of the miners' strike early in 1963. But the trade unions soon discovered their weakness in any ordinary strike and, like the peasants and in time even the students, they gradually reverted from mass agitation to ordinary political lobbying.[6] As Parliament regained some of its lost functions, the morale of its members improved somewhat from the disastrous level of 1961.

Pompidou had over Debré the advantage not merely of a more loyal majority, but also of a franker opposition. For once fighting had ended in Algeria and the threat of civil war disappeared in France, the critics no longer felt inhibited from attacking the author as well as the executant of policy. The pretence that the President was merely an arbiter was abandoned at last, and he was accepted as a great political leader subject to ordinary political criticism. In the 1962 election he recognized the new situation and frankly appealed for a UNR victory. In the new Parliament, therefore, the government saw better prospects for useful collaboration with its majority, and the majority had a new incentive for loyalty to the government: having gone into the election campaign expecting only disaster as their recompense, they had come out of it with sixty more seats than before. Realizing that the voters had shown their approval of stable government as well as the President's policies, they were naturally encouraged in their 'unconditional' support for both. For at last the French electorate seemed ready, like the British, to vote for or against their national leadership and to expect their representatives to keep it in power—rather than turn it out whenever some sudden crisis or unpopular reform offended an interest in the country and a marginal group in the Assembly.

(II) THE INFLUENCE OF THE MAJORITY

The government now began to take more pains to organize its relations with its parliamentary followers. Debré, for all his long parliamentary experience, was always bad at managing his supporters (and worse with

[6]The government handled the miners most ineptly, offended public opinion and had to retreat. But subsequent strikes forfeited public sympathy: cf. above, p. 89.

opponents): partly because with his rigorous and self-righteous temperament he thought patronage an unworthy device, and found criticism hard to bear; partly because of the natural difficulties of defending a policy in which he notoriously half-disbelieved; and partly because, more than once, his own willingness to meet the wishes of the National Assembly was vetoed by the President.[7] Pompidou, who had no parliamentary past and was not even a member of the UNR, had to go out of his way to make up for these handicaps. Although his first attempt to broaden the government's parliamentary base was foiled, Pompidou, unlike Debré, took very nearly all his ministers from Parliament;[8] and it was from his advent that ministers came to regard themselves without pretence as representing the constituencies they had nominally renounced on taking office.

While the parliamentarians were flattered by the choice of new ministers from their ranks, the UNR backbenchers were given a more effective voice.[9] There were of course many informal contacts among Gaullists, for many of their ministers and prominent parliamentarians had been personal friends or political associates on first-name terms for twenty years or more. Members were invited to occasional lunches with the prime minister, the parliamentary party had an annual weekend meeting outside Paris, and as in all legislatures there were irregular contacts in the lobbies and at meals and receptions. Moreover, the formal machinery for keeping ministers in touch with their majority was greatly improved. Only one chairman of the UNR parliamentary party had hitherto held the post for more than a year, and the party had displayed some resentment at the pressures exercised by the leadership on its choice.[10] But Henri Rey, elected in 1963, remained as chairman throughout that Parliament to the general satisfaction of the members. He worked with vice-chairmen elected by their

[7]Perhaps over the recall of Parliament in March 1960, certainly over the censure motion in the special session of September 1961, when Article 16 was still in force.

[8]He kept only three 'technicians', Couve de Murville (Foreign Affairs), Messmer (Defence) and Joxe, who had been a Gaullist for years (Administrative Reform). (All three stood for Parliament in 1967; only Joxe was elected.) At the 1966 reshuffle only one of the nine new ministers was not taken from Parliament and in 1967 all the eight newcomers were.

On Pompidou's first ministry see above, p. 26.

[9]The next seven paragraphs are partly based on J. Charlot, *L'UNR: Etude du pouvoir au sein d'un parti politique* (Paris 1967), Ch. 6.

[10]Hence perhaps the big vote (a third) for the right-wing extremist J. B. Biaggi against Louis Terrenoire in 1959; hence certainly the victory of Raymond Schmittlein over André Valabrègue in 1960, and his two renominations. At least the UNR chairman mattered—in RPF days the post had no authority at all, apparently for fear it might become a focus for rivalry with the President of the RPF, Charles de Gaulle.

colleagues, instead of insisting like some of his predecessors on choosing his own.

In the second Parliament the leadership, which cherished the Jacobin conception of the Republic one and indivisible, reluctantly agreed to seat the UNR deputies in the chamber according to their constituencies, and to organize a kind of regional whip system (not unlike that of parties in the British House of Commons or the United States House of Representatives) which facilitated communications within the parliamentary party.[11] The 'whips' in this case were the twenty-two elected members of its committee, the *bureau politique,* who sat weekly together with the party leaders;[12] it kept in close touch with the government, and firmly organized the Tuesday afternoon meetings of the whole parliamentary party in the Salle Colbert, the largest room in the Palais Bourbon. These meetings were frequently addressed by ministers, including the prime minister himself. In the first Parliament many were very stormy, notably over the church schools bill in 1959; in the second they were less agitated, though Michel Debré celebrated his election to the Assembly by leading a vigorous attack in the Salle Colbert on the government's bill to recognize conscientious objection to military service, and by pressing successfully for many mean-spirited amendments.

The junior minister responsible for relations with Parliament attended the *bureau politique* regularly from 1963. Like a British chief whip, he warned the cabinet when its followers were showing signs of uneasiness—or even of indignation running so high that ministers would have to make concessions. For Gaullist politicians were responsive like others to their constituents' demands. During the 1963 miners' strike, UNR deputies and senators from Lorraine tried to maintain communications between the government and the miners, and twice visited the prime minister to express their concern. In the debate on the amnesty for OAS rebels and terrorists in April 1966, the government with Communist help—and despite the defection of the Republican Independents—defeated strong pressure from all the Fourth Republican parties to release all the prisoners. But while only eighteen out of 230 UNR deputies failed to support the government, these abstainers included seven of the nine members from the Mediterranean coast where the Algerian settler refugees have clustered.[13] However, normally discipline was effective without being rigid: individual abstentions were not uncommon, though large-scale defections were rare. Sanctions were applied only rarely, reluctantly and on great

[11]Charlot, pp. 152–3, 168–9.
[12]These ex-officio members might number as many as thirty, but most—the ministers—never came. See Charlot, pp. 176–82, on ministers' relations with their followers.
[13]Eight months nearer the election most of them had moved from abstention to opposition on this issue: *Monde* 24–25 April and 15 December 1966.

occasions. For the UNR deputies, like British MPs, usually voted with the government because they believed in its policies or because their constituents had sent them to Parliament to support it, and not merely because they were whipped.

Contrary to their opponents' belief, this 'unconditional' backing by no means indicated tame acquiescence in all the government did. Bills were often altered to satisfy UNR criticism, sometimes before they came before Parliament, like the great agriculture act of 1962, and sometimes in the house itself, for example a bill on motor insurance in 1966. Many ministers made a real effort to minimize difficulties by consulting the party, or at least those members interested in the subject, in advance of legislation.[14] This was only prudent, for particularly in the second Parliament majority members monopolized almost all the important positions on the Assembly's standing committees, and a minister who neglected to discuss matters with the chairman or rapporteur might find him making trouble on the floor of the house. Sometimes when feeling in the UNR ranks was strong, its spokesman would take the lead in criticism, as André Fanton obliged the government to produce more money for compensating the victims of OAS bomb attacks in 1963. On other occasions the committee representatives would express the uneasiness of the house as a whole—often demonstrated also through threatened defection by the Republican Independents. Where the cabinet stood firm, as on the State Security Court bill early in 1963, even so influential a figure as René Capitant, chairman of the legislation committee, could only give voice to his doubts and settle for relatively minor concessions. But where feeling was strong and the government open to persuasion, they might win a substantial compromise, as when Joël Le Theule and the defence committee reshaped the military service bill of 1965. Every year it was Gaullist rapporteurs—especially Louis Vallon—who brought forward the most informed, incisive and damaging criticisms of the budget.[15] Like British MPs, after saying what they thought, they voted with their party. It does not follow (in either case) that the criticisms go unheeded.

When opinion was running high, either in the house as a whole or among UNR members in particular, a prudent minister would without undue publicity make concessions in committee. If he did not—

[14]'How do things work in day-to-day politics ? Before a bill . . . is presented, the minister concerned comes to explain it to the majority members . . . If the minister and the majority cannot agree, it is normal practice for the prime minister to come in his turn to try to settle the points in dispute . . . If conciliation proves impossible, the government may withdraw its bill . . .': René Sanson (UNR deputy), *Monde* 4 Oct. 1966.

[15]Charlot, pp. 166–8; Avril, *Régime* (2nd ed.), pp. 387–8, who attributes the fact to the superior information available to government supporters. (On members' problems over information see Chandernagor, pp. 171–5.)

and some ministers, particularly those without parliamentary experience, were prone to intransigence—then the rebels and the rapporteur
had various channels open to them. If the criticisms were widespread,
the Republican Independents might be quietly reassured that their
defection from the majority—in committee or in the house—would
not be greatly resented by their UNR colleagues, whatever the government might feel. If the irritation was particularly strong within the
UNR's own ranks, its spokesman could take it to the party meeting
or, in the first instance, to the *bureau politique*. If he convinced his
colleagues there, his hand was greatly strengthened, for the chairman
of the parliamentary party would accompany him to discuss with the
minister an amendment or a protest which was now put forward in
the name of the party as a whole. This line of communication, however, could not readily be used to bring subjects to the attention of
the party—and therefore of the government—in advance of a ministerial decision to deal with them. For these the ground had to be
prepared beforehand, and this was the main role of the UNR's subject
groups.[16]

These groups resembled those of a British parliamentary party in
many ways, not least in their diversity. Some were far more active
than others and, among the active ones, the degree of influence they
exerted varied greatly. They differed according to the nature of the
subject with which they dealt, the extent to which UNR deputies
agreed—and cared—about it, the energy and the strategy of their
back-bench organizer, and the character and purposes of the minister
concerned. Through them some radical members of the government,
such as Edgard Pisani at Agriculture and Gilbert Grandval at Labour,
mobilized support for their proposed reforms against the resistance of
their colleagues (especially of course the finance minister) or their
civil servants. The half-dozen active subject groups kept in regular
contact with the major interests in their field, invited their spokesmen
for hearings, questioned the minister on their proposals, and sometimes promoted bills of their own. The agricultural group persuaded
the party to sponsor a private member's bill on contracts for farmers'
supplies or products, which passed into law in 1964. The labour group
had one Left Gaullist, René Capitant, as chairman and from 1962 to
1965 another (Grandval) as minister; it inspired two government bills
of some importance, one to increase the powers of works committees
in factories, the other to extend social security insurance to self-
employed workers. But as this subject group consisted of those Gaullists most interested in social questions, which were not a major
preoccupation of the party, it was not altogether representative of the
UNR deputies as a whole. Both its bills aroused much resentment:
the first was criticized by some UNR members and all their Republican

[16]On these groups see Charlot, pp. 153–66, 182.

Independent allies, and had to be imposed by a package vote in which the opposition rallied to the government against a section of the majority; the second, though widely welcomed generally, was vigorously attacked on the floor by several Gaullist doctor MPs.

The negative role of the subject groups was at least equally important, for they could mobilize party opinion against a measure as well as for one. Thus the agriculture group obliged Pisani to withdraw a bill on land law reform, which conservatives feared as a potential threat to property, while the sub-committee on fiscal matters succeeded in delaying and modifying the bill introducing the value-added tax— a warning the government should have heeded more than it did when, two years later, after revising the details to appease the sub-committee but without making nearly sufficient effort to prepare the parliamentary ground, it finally brought that luckless measure before the Assembly.[17] But though a few of the subject groups could thus play a real role in expressing party feelings to the government, many were inactive. Sometimes their official organizer preferred to use the regular standing committee. Sometimes their objectives met with resistance within the party itself: the regional development group succumbed to discouragement when its proposals to limit the growth of Paris were successfully opposed by the strong Parisian contingent of UNR deputies. Sometimes they lost heart at their inability to overcome the universal stumbling-block, the ministry of finance.

Until January 1966 this vital ministry, never yet held by a member of the UNR, was bitterly criticized within the party. Its policies caused constant tension between the UNR, especially its small but vocal left wing, and the Republican Independents—whose votes gave the Gaullists a majority in the Assembly and whose men, in UNR eyes, were over-represented in the government. The feelings were reciprocated; soon after their leader Giscard d'Estaing was evicted from the finance ministry, a prominent RI deputy described his friends' role within the majority 'as rather like that of France within the Atlantic alliance'.[18] But though temperament, conviction and interest often separated the two parties, the Republican Independents fulfilled an important parliamentary function for the Gaullist majority. It was through them that the leadership was warned when the rest of the house felt strongly that the government was abusing its authority—as over the State Security Court and, with more effect, on the amnesty for 'political' offenders. It was also through the RI that doubts within the UNR ranks, whether on the substance of policy or on its electoral repercussions, could be conveyed to the responsible authorities without compromising the doubters' reputations for loyalty. A few—or even many—RI abstentions would not bring the government down

[17]See above, p. 93.
[18]André Moynet, Monde 21 April 1966.

but they acted as a useful alarm signal. UNR members might resent the greater independence of their allies, especially when the RI became potential competitors before the 1967 election, but they were sometimes glad of an indirect channel of protest to the government. Some of them even regarded the RI as a useful guarantee of their own independent influence, and feared that if the UNR ever won a clear majority in the Assembly, ministers would wield the whip more ruthlessly and show less consideration for the views of their followers.

These fears were perhaps ill-founded, for after 1962 greater parliamentary security had made the government more, not less, receptive to the views of majority members. Besides enjoying more encouragement and consideration than in the past, they now had access to patronage outside the walls of Parliament and a favoured position within them. Once the austere Debré era was over, the new regional planning machinery as well as the old resources of the central administration were employed, fairly discreetly but still on a substantial scale, to buttress the ministry's friends in local and national government.[19] In the constituencies the member (or candidate) of the majority was allowed, as in the United States, to announce good tidings about government grants or contracts.

In the Assembly itself Gaullists enjoyed many privileges. Their private members' bills and oral questions had more chance of consideration, at least in the second Parliament (there was not much discrimination in the first). When an opposition amendment was too popular to resist, the minister would sometimes encourage a UNR deputy to put down a similar amendment and take the political credit, the government granting to its friends what it had refused to its opponents. The majority took every seat on conference committees with the Senate, and monopolized Parliament's representation on some outside bodies— notably taking all its four seats on the ORTF council which was supposed to scrutinize the impartiality of the State broadcasting and television service! In the second Assembly the majority took over all the standing committee chairmanships and presented the reports on all major bills. This was reasonable enough;[20] but there was no

[19]Its enemies were not starved: that would have been too ostentatious and might have provoked the electorate, as Maurice Herzog found in the March 1965 municipal election. (This junior minister hinted that as mayor of Lyons he would enjoy official goodwill not available to the incumbent—who utterly crushed him by exploiting the Lyonnais' resentment at this illegitimate pressure from Paris.) But a Gaullist candidate in Limousin, where their hopes of an electoral breakthrough were highest, claimed that the area had recently had a disproportionate share of government money, and more exceptional grants than any other region: *Monde*, 6 Dec. 1966.

[20]As pro-Gaullists outside the UNR were not excluded, Maurice Schumann remained chairman of the foreign affairs committee. (The most vociferous traditionalists, the Socialists, had themselves taken two-thirds of the committee chairs in 1956, when they were under a hundred strong.)

corresponding change in the established practice by which debating time was allocated between government, committee, majority and opposition, although in the new dispensation this gave the Gaullists three shares and all the opposing parties together only one.[21] It was not the opposition alone which was unable or unwilling to adapt itself to the new situation.

Above all the majority had the satisfaction of being able to influence policy, at least in domestic affairs. They could bring successful pressure to bear for bills to be introduced, like the amnesty for political offenders which the minister refused in November 1964 and presented in December; or modified before they were brought forward, like the agriculture act of 1962 or the bill to regulate broadcasting; or amended in the house, like the pensions code, the value-added tax, the State security court bill, or the agriculture acts again; or delayed, like the conscientious objection bill; or withdrawn and improved, like the measure for settling refugees from North Africa. UNR members were consulted and favoured after 1962, Republican Independents were represented in the government and endowed with some bargaining power. The other parties were more frustrated, for—like the opposition in the House of Commons—they had no weapon but argument. If the majority remained disciplined, the government could always win. And its solidarity remained proof against the most skilful manoeuvres to chip it away—especially as the new rules of procedure had been specially devised to deny the critics any opportunity to chip.

(III) THE GOVERNMENT'S CRITICS

It was the moderates in the opposition who suffered most. They could not amend in detail policies they broadly accepted, because the government could stop them with a package vote. They could not follow French parliamentary custom and their own inclinations by voting for the budget and defence estimates, each in its single package, without Gaullists claiming that they were approving the nuclear deterrent, and fulsomely welcoming their 'journey to Canossa'.[22] They were unwilling to vote for the government without being able to explain their differences from it, and unable to choose their own ground for expressing those differences because it allowed so few votes—not even, for example, on its own declarations of foreign policy. Their only outlet was to propose a motion of censure, and this was a weapon which moderate critics, by definition, disliked using.

For the all-out opponents of the government the problem was

---

[21]Avril, *Régime*, 2nd ed., p. 387; P. Viansson-Ponté in *Monde*, 21 Dec. 1963. Cf. above, p. 78.

[22]Hamon and Emeri, *RDP* 80.1 (Jan. 1964), p. 88.

different. Their attacks had little prospect of arousing an echo in the ranks of the majority, and their aim, like that of a British opposition, was to use Parliament not as a terrain for persuasion or manoeuvre but as a sounding-board for appealing to the country. But here, too, they were frustrated by the difficulty of forcing a vote at any time, or a debate at a moment when their attacks on some ministerial misdeed might have had some popular resonance. The conventions of French political behaviour did nothing to deter the majority from exploiting all its new advantages.[23] Television was controlled by the Gaullists and often, especially up to 1965, was shamelessly exploited. The press usually gave little attention to debates in a Parliament without prestige, which no longer overthrew a cabinet every few months and was therefore assumed to be futile by the very people who had condemned its frenzied activity in the past.

Thus the opposition parties had little political opportunity to persuade the majority, and little procedural opportunity to arouse public opinion against it through Parliament; and they were disconcerted by the new situation in which majorities never split and governments never fell. In this state of disillusionment the absenteeism which had always flourished, and was bad enough even in the Gaullist ranks, became endemic among the opposition parties and especially among their leaders. Their spokesmen complained in private of the impossibility of persuading their rank and file colleagues to do serious parliamentary work.[24] But the example came from above, and the best-known names—Pflimlin, Mollet, even Defferre—came rarely to the Assembly and by no means always spoke even in major debates. Indeed François Mitterrand earned much of his reputation by his skill, initiative and imagination in seizing every opportunity for expoiting Gaullist faults—and merits—to impede and embarrass the President and all his ministers, followers and policies.

Whatever the frustrations of opposition deputies, their colleagues in the upper house found their situation far more exasperating still. With their secure majority, the senatorial opposition could always win the battle, never the war. Matters became worse than ever in the second Parliament when, because of the feud between de Gaulle and Monnerville, cabinet ministers generally refused to speak in the Senate and left their juniors to defend the government there. Moreover, when an important bill had passed the Assembly on a package vote, the minister of state in charge of it would often ask for one in the Senate also. But whereas the government would have discussed with the deputies of the majority what changes it could accept, the senators were simply informed at the very beginning of the debate that their

[23]As when the government cheated over its measures against alcoholism: above, p. 88.

[24]Cf. Chandernagor, pp. 93, 155-7, 159.

amendments would not even be voted on.[25] Increasingly they showed
their irritation by rejecting major government bills, which were then
passed over their heads.[26] This merely persuaded the government
that nothing could be done with them, so that both sides felt a sense
of justified grievance and communications between them grew steadily
worse.

Yet the Senate had no real wish to oppose systematically or obstruct
deliberately. The opposition senators elect, without reciprocity,
one UNR colleague to most conference committees; and when the
minister of the interior did them the courtesy of piloting his bill
reforming the administration of the Paris region, they repaid the com-
pliment by passing it. Their moderation was partly inspired by the hope
of reconciliation (many who would not repudiate Monnerville hoped
he would retire voluntarily), and partly by their consciousness of
weakness: for while their resistance could never stop a bill passing
into law, it might provoke de Gaulle into another amendment of the
constitution directed against their house. Consequently the second
chamber, which in 1959 had seemed to the Left alarmingly powerful,
exercised perhaps less influence on controversial legislation in the
Fifth Republic than ever before in its history.

On questions which were not central to the political conflict, however, the new institutions worked well. The senators' voice was heard
and listened to on bills of a juridical and technical nature which were
sometimes of great social importance. On such matters effective cooperation was possible, and was achieved, between the two houses,
between ministers and backbenchers, and between majority and
opposition.[27] After 1963 many secondary bills and a few major ones
passed unopposed or even with all-party support. This was possible
only because the Communists, for the first time, had become a party
of discriminating instead of total opposition.[28] But it also indicated
that many of the government's reforms were useful and acceptable.

The improvement of Parliament's legislative performance was no
doubt partly due to Debré's constitutional straitjacket. But this could
not transform French members into British ones, and if traditional
political irresponsibility was less frequently and obviously displayed,
it still lay not far from the surface. When the constitution required

[25]Goguel in *Projet* 13 (March 1967), p. 288n.
[26]Above, p. 70. Even on a fairly minor bill against usury, the Assembly over-
rode the Senate's amendments by show of hands, unanimously and without
debate: *Monde*, 16 Dec. 1966.
[27]As over the adoption bill: above, p. 96. For Parliament's influence on
different types of bill see Goguel, *loc. cit.*, pp. 289–99.
[28]And because Communist amendments were sometimes accepted by the
majority. One, on the military service bill, transformed the method of dealing
with cases of family hardship.

secret voting the majority was as unreliable as ever.[29] The UNR occasionally matched the worst performances of the old parties: on the amnesty for common-law offences in 1966, a UNR spokesman made repeated and ingenious efforts to extend its benefits surreptitiously to his party colleague Pierre Lemarchand (recently disbarred as a by-product of the Ben Barka scandal); though the government and the committee chairman (Capitant) joined the opposition and the Republican Independents against him, all but twenty UNR members voted with him amid scenes recalling the old days at their very worst —and he lost only by 255 to 208.[30] When a popular cause came up the house would still, as in the past, sometimes vote almost unanimously against ministers, for instance in 1964 on commercial leaseholds, on the pensions code, and on the treatment of civil servants returning from North Africa.[31] The TVA debate in December 1965 showed that Gaullist ministers and members, like their predecessors, were subject both to the individual constituency pressures and to the natural fears of the nation's government falling into dangerous hands after the next election, which explained the behaviour of Fourth Republican politicians far more often than the defects of personal character which Gaullist critics had been so ready to denounce.[32]

In spite of these aberrations the second Parliament played a much more constructive role than the first, and this was mainly due to the UNR. On almost all major occasions it gave loyal and sometimes courageous support to the government. In addition—and not always with happy results—it sometimes furnished the effective opposition from within its own ranks, like a British party (Labour after 1945, Conservatives after 1959) when a great victory has just weakened and discouraged the other side. The regular opposition contributed little, but the reasons were only in part those which applied in these cases in Britain. For the new rules, which prevented Parliament being used as a forum for manoeuvres to divide the majority, also enabled that majority to hamper its opponents in criticizing the government and appealing to the country as a skilful Opposition Front Bench can at Westminster. The opposition parties were demoralized by electoral defeat and internal division, and frustrated by their inability to find a role in the new parliamentary situation. This was partly because they were slow to adapt but partly also because the new masters gave them little opportunity to play any useful part. As a Gaullist senator who was also a constitutional expert put it in 1965, the government's misuse

[29]During 1963 the Assembly could find no majority to elect the High Court of Justice which tries political cases: *Monde*, 1 Jan. 1964. For a similar case in 1952 see Williams, *Crisis and Compromise*, p. 300.

[30]*JO* 27 and 28 April 1966, pp. 965–6, 997–1003; *Monde*, 29 and 30 April 1966.

[31]*Monde*, 27 June, 9 Oct., 16 and 17 Dec. 1964.

[32]On this incident see above, pp. 94–5.

of its powers 'is leading to an unbalance which is the reverse of that which we rightly condemned [in the past]. If this goes any further there will soon be no representative assemblies remaining but only symbolic ones'.[33]

[33]M. Prélot, preface to Guichard-Ayoub *et al.*, *op. cit.*, p. viii.

VIII

The New Model Parliament

The makers of the 1958 constitution set out to cure the traditional bad habits of French parliamentarians by importing, mainly from Britain, institutions they understood very imperfectly in detail and not at all in spirit. Major policy decisions were transferred to a President who owed no responsibility to Parliament, gloried in his direct contact with the electorate through referendums and provincial tours, and made no secret of his dislike and contempt for the intermediaries. His example was followed by his ministers, many of whom had never sat in the Parliament from which they were now constitutionally excluded. At first they had no secure majority there, and regarded their nominal supporters (not to mention the opposition) with undisguised suspicion. Parliament's morale declined with its prestige. Members—especially those of the opposition parties—were far less assiduous than their predecessors, and many other bad habits still flourished unimpaired. With no disciplined majority in the first Assembly, rigid rules proved an inadequate substitute; with such a majority in the second, they seemed irksome and unnecessary.

Gaullists maintained that the restrictions were essential to avoid a return to the bad old days. Parliament in the Third and Fourth Republics, they contended, was neither representative nor efficient: the politicians were wholly engrossed in making and unmaking governments with no reference to the general public, while constant cabinet crises precluded the governmental leadership without which the deputies could not organize their own business. Parliament enjoyed full formal sovereignty which it was incapable of exercising—except destructively. The new regime gives it a role which is more confined on paper, but more useful in reality. The Parliament of the Fifth Republic will not only be more efficient than its predecessors, but more representative too. This case deserves serious examination.

There are several ways to assess how far a Parliament represents the people. When their members were first called together as a check on the power of a monarch who ruled independently of them, they were sent as agents of their communities to put forward the views and defend the interests of their constituents. By this test the French Parliament before 1958 had been fully representative, since every minor local or economic interest had its voice in Assembly and Senate.[1] But the criterion was without merit in the eyes of de Gaulle, with his mystique of 'the higher interest of France' and his contempt for 'the immediate advantage of Frenchmen',[2] or of Debré with his Jacobin devotion to the nation and his hatred of pressure-groups. Nor was it only Gaullists who felt that once the government became responsible to Parliament, the traditional representative function must play a less predominant part; the legislature could no longer remain primarily a market-place where groups bargained and negotiated.[3]

The reaction went too far in the first Assembly, which was widely mistrusted as a stronghold of the war party both by loyal Gaullists and by many opposition leaders. The cabinet and administration neglected the parliamentary arena, and pressure-groups therefore soon deserted it to lobby in the ministries or protest in the streets. But by 1962 the war was over and the government, with a secure majority and more conciliatory leadership, showed less suspicion of Parliament. Members resumed their 'representative' functions with undiminished vigour, and today towns and regions make full use of the parliamentary channel to defend their cause against Paris—and against each other. Local complaints drown all other sounds when the national Plan is debated, and interest-group spokesmen are heard in every economic discussion in the house or in committee. But these pressures remain far less effective than they were before 1958, for on many matters the administration can act without consulting the legislature, and the minister's position is now much stronger even when Parliament cannot be by-passed. Many negotiations therefore go on directly between the administration and the pressure-groups without being mediated through Parliament at all. The decline of its representative function is thus a significant factor in its loss of importance and prestige.

Another common criterion of the 'representativeness' of a Parliament is the extent to which it contains a fair cross-section of the whole people. No legislature is ever likely to meet this test completely, for the better-educated, better-off, more articulate sections of the population are over-represented everywhere. But the distortion was always particularly marked in France, where professional men were dominant and few members came from the main economic occupations —industry, commerce, agriculture. There were very few workers until

[1] Even more so before 1940, when the weakness of organized pressure-groups accentuated Parliament's representative role. Cf. Chandernagor, p. 113.

[2] C. de Gaulle, *Mémoires de Guerre* III: *Le Salut* (Paris 1959), pp. 28, 43.

[3] 'The member represents his constituency, not France . . . we have no National Assembly but two Senates representing local interests . . .': André Philip, *Monde* 15 Sept. 1962. This Left Socialist later became a Gaullist.

1936, and as the new electoral system damages the Communist party, working-class representation has fallen to a much lower level in the Fifth Republic than in the Fourth. But the type of middle-class deputy has significantly changed—the Senate remaining, as always, a stronghold of the old order. The Gaullist successes in the Assembly brought in younger men, and more businessmen, managers and administrators at the expense of teachers, journalists and lawyers (but not of doctors). MRP recruited some young peasant leaders, very different from the older and wealthier spokesmen of agriculture in the past. These changes give more weight to the outlook and experience of professions and age-groups which are playing a growing role in the country's life.

Thirdly, there is the criterion of Gaullist theorists: the extent to which Parliament represents what the general public thinks and wants.[4] In this sense it was plainly deficient in the past, for though the politician often engaged in his battles and manoeuvres because of the demands of voters in the country, those voters neither understood nor approved the methods by which their member fought for their claims and interests. They chose him, not to sustain a government, but to defend a pressure-group, a locality, or an ideological position; then, when this defence led him to bring down a government, the same voters condemned him for his selfish irresponsibility (or rather condemned his colleagues, for though politicians as a whole were thoroughly unpopular, most people made an exception for their own member). The Fifth Republic has not resolved but reversed this contradiction in their attitude. In providing stable government it has met a demand which was latent but deep-seated, and at successive general elections and referendums the electorate has shown its gratitude to the Gaullists and its suspicion that the old parties were bent on bringing back the old system. But while Frenchmen are better represented as citizens, they are worse represented as members of particular groups. In one respect they are more satisfied, and the regime gains prestige. In the other they are more discontented, and Parliament loses it. Few ordinary Frenchmen believe their Parliament plays any useful role in the system, and the reputation of parties and politicians suffers from this scepticism.[5] The Gaullist members are thought as impotent to influence policy as their opponents, for they never defeat the government and rarely show open disagreement with it. This 'unconditional' discipline, for which the majority has been so widely mocked, is the necessary foundation for the governmental stability which is so widely appreciated. But the link is not detected because

[4]See above, p. 20. De Gaulle's own criterion is different.
[5]In March 1966 an opinion poll found 43% wanting the role of Parliament to be more important, 3% less, 29% the same; 25% did not know. Corresponding figures for the parties were 25, 20, 30 and 27%. Since 1962 all polls have produced very similar results (except one in 1965 which found the parties more popular and Parliament less): *Sondages* 1966, no. 1, p. 38.

of the strong tradition that democracy means opposition to authority: Parliament is seen as 'representative' when it stands for the people against the powers that be; it can be made efficient for government only by losing its representative character. The criteria of political judgment are rarely free from ambiguity.

The criterion of efficiency is no exception, for it can be sought for different purposes which determine the role expected of an efficient Parliament: as an electoral college, a legislative machine, or an instrument for exerting public pressure on the authorities. In choosing a government the old French Parliament carried out rather badly much the same operation as the House of Commons of the generation for which Bagehot wrote in 1867. But within a few years British society and politics had changed; party discipline had transformed the normal role of Parliament into one of sustaining and influencing the ministry rather than choosing it, and had ensured that the choice was made at the polls and not in the house. Nearly a century later the same changes have taken place across the Channel. Instead of spending much of their time and most of their energy in making and unmaking ministries, the first two Parliaments of the Fifth Republic ejected only a single government, and members discovered that loyalty to the men in office could pay electoral dividends. Cabinet crises were in the old regime the only (if an unsatisfactory) way of forcing Parliament, or rather the marginal party within it, to take distasteful decisions on dangerous problems. In the new system, that need is met by other means, and the function of choosing and maintaining a government is —by twentieth century standards—far better performed. There is, however, a serious reservation. The old Parliament, for all its faults, was a splendid nursery of ministerial talent. But many of the older generation have died, retired or suffered defeat, and deputies with governmental experience are becoming rare. Although since 1962 nearly all ministers are again chosen from Parliament, until recently few returned to it when they lost office.[6] Its low prestige damages the recruitment of able newcomers, and its limited opportunities and low morale discourage assiduity. On the other hand the Third and Fourth Republics, especially in their last years, not only produced but also consumed able politicians at an enormous rate; if fewer men of ministerial timber have been discovered in the Fifth, fewer have been needed. And in diverting members' attention from the endless struggle to bring down and replace the government of the day, the Gaullists have achieved one clear and perhaps decisive advantage for the new Parliament.

A second success is in its efficient functioning as a legislative

[6]Michel Debré was a notable exception; and lately the practice has changed. Of nine ministers dropped in January 1966, six stood at the next election and five won; of seven dropped in April 1967, five retain seats in the Assembly.

machine. A far larger programme of major legislation can be handled
now that its scope has been limited by the removal of minor matters
to the domain of regulations, its procedure streamlined by the concentration of leadership in the hands of the government, and its character
transformed by the appearance of a disciplined majority. The old
device of delegating legislative power to the government, which had
to be used whenever a large or politically difficult measure was introduced, has not disappeared altogether but, apart from the peculiar
problems of Algeria, it was extremely rare in the first two Parliaments.[7] Of course the new system is far from perfect. The package
vote procedure makes it all too easy for ministers to reject reasonable
criticisms, and for members to support them without having to take
responsibility for the consequences. The second chamber problem
is still unresolved, for while the machinery works smoothly, the political quarrel leads the deputies often to ignore the contribution which
the senators could make. But today, as in the past, the senators might
have retained more influence by accepting governmental measures in
principle and trying to improve them in detail. Often they have
chosen frustration by insisting instead on expressing the opinions of
the political opposition, without having the power to enforce their
views. Yet despite its weaknesses and abuses the new system ensures
that legislative leadership remains in the hands of the government and
that real opportunities for criticism and even resistance are open to
the members, especially the majority members. As a result the legislative function of the French Parliament is better performed than it ever
was in the past.

In other ways Parliament is less efficient. Restrictions have been
imposed to stop the harassing tactics of obstructive pressure-groups
and ambitious challengers of the reigning ministry, but these limitations seriously impede Parliament's debating and deliberative functions. The rules confine criticism to oral questions which are usually
futile, and motions of censure which cannot be frequent. The practice
shows little appreciation of the balance, indispensable to any real
Parliament, between the government's need to get its business through
and the opposition's claim to deploy its case effectively: the critics
cannot force a debate at the right moment, or a vote at all. Consequently Parliament is sadly inefficient as a forum for popular grievances, as a check on the administration, as a defender of the liberties
of the subject, or as a political sounding-board for the opposition
(or indeed government) to appeal to the electorate. Low morale within
and low prestige without further react on its ability to perform any of
its functions. Past traditions must bear much of the blame for this
situation—and for the rigidity of the constitution-makers. The responsibility is shared by an opposition which has become too easily and too

[7]See above, p. 73.

completely discouraged. But it lies most heavily on the men holding the power and enjoying all the advantages of the new system, who could well have afforded to interpret the new rules far more liberally.

For the second Parliament approached Westminster conditions in many ways. The upper house, with time at its disposal, was often able to improve bills technically and sometimes could focus public criticism, but could never get its way against the solid ministerial majority, and was wary of provoking a threat to its own composition, powers or existence by insisting on its full legal rights. For in the lower house the government had a secure majority with which it kept in constant touch, and to which it often made concessions, usually minor but occasionally important. Whenever possible ministers and their supporters reached agreement behind the scenes; a public row occurred from time to time but was rarely an effective way of changing the government's mind. Members from the majority party expressed their views freely and often critically, but voted for the government at the end of the debate—now and then abstaining when disagreement went deep, but hardly ever voting with the opposition. There was some justification for the Gaullists' proud claim to have introduced stern British political virtues into a chaotic Assembly while the Fourth Republican parties stayed sunk in self-indulgent futility. The UNR members have often shown much better discipline and more political courage than most French parties, while their opponents have been conspicuously slow to shake off past habits and find a useful role for the new Parliament to play.[8] Many complaints were indeed mere expressions of nostalgia for the old regime, and of resentment at the government's authority and the government's majority.

There were, of course, some major differences between Westminster and Paris. The Senate was less conciliatory than the modern House of Lords because it was less detached from the ordinary party struggle. In the House of Commons an impartial Speaker rules on disputes between majority and opposition and ensures equal (indeed favoured) treatment for minority views. Private members' time is limited but, through the crude machinery of the ballot, everyone has the same chance of profiting from it. Nearly all opposition members owe allegiance to a single coherent alternative government, which has frequent opportunities for determining the subject of debate, and can insist on a vote whenever it thinks fit. It can neither harry nor obstruct, except within narrow limits, and it can win its point only by persuading the government; nevertheless it retains an effective and not merely theoretical right to use Parliament as a forum for appealing to the electorate.

The real difference is in attitudes rather than institutions. At Westminster ministers are themselves MPs, and are selected largely accord-

[8]But see next note.

ing to their reputation among their colleagues, whose views are supposed to be reflected in the policies on which they decide. But in
Paris major policies are determined at the Elysée. Most ministers,
even today, have never sat on the back benches and only a minority
have attained office through their parliamentary performance. The
cabinet does not have to represent the leaders and factions of the
parliamentary majority, while the various opposition parties are deeply
divided among themselves.[9] Ministers take so little account of Parliament that they have even presented the budget to the television
audience before the deputies. They allow members to be represented
on sixty advisory committees—but rarely on the ones that matter.[10]
As René Pleven has said, they rarely give the impression of liking
contact with the members or recognizing its value.[11]

The analogy with the House of Commons, so much favoured among
Gaullists, is thus largely valid in form but partly false in reality.
While some complaints against the new regime do express mere
nostalgia for the past, others are justifiable protests against the abuse
by the new masters of the unprecedented powers they now enjoy.
The French political arena has never been conspicuous for fair play,
and here the Fifth Republic has made little change and no improvement. Like so many of their predecessors, most Gaullists have preferred short-term party advantage to the long-term strategy of making
the new institutions acceptable to all serious politicians.[12] Although
these institutions have repeatedly been approved by the electorate,
their misuse could still bring about the reaction which, in France,
has regularly rebuked the temporary victor who abuses his triumph.

Yet in 1967 the limits of probable constitutional change seem much
narrower than they did eight years earlier. The old regime is now
almost certainly past restoring, while Parliament is unlikely to sink
back into the neglect and impotence of the early years of the reign.
During that brief period, dominated by the Algerian conflict, the war
party in the Assembly was willing to use any instrument to undermine
the President and frustrate the policy which he was pursuing with
popular support. Even apart from these exceptional circumstances,
Algeria proved to de Gaulle that he could not rule France as an
arbiter above the ordinary political battle, intervening only occasionally to lay down the course of policy. For in that role he was frustrated
by his own administration, army and even ministers. Instead he had

[9]In 1966 François Mitterrand formed a 'shadow cabinet' of the non-Communist Left; it was a significant pointer to the new public demand for a choice
between alternative governments, but did not make credible its claim to provide
one.

[10]Chandernagor, pp. 115–21.

[11]In his local paper, quoted *Monde* 11–12 Aug. 1963.

[12]Since these words were written the demand for special legislative powers in
economic and social matters (above, p. 28n.) has provided a striking example.

to become the active head of his own government, and therefore a
great political leader of unusually wide appeal, rather than a national
figurehead. This change was foreshadowed by every referendum, for
the President always warned that he would resign if the result was
unsatisfactory. It was ratified in 1962 by the constitutional amendment providing that presidents should be elected by direct popular
vote. It was firmly established by the 1965 presidential election, when
every serious candidate campaigned as the leader of a potential political majority; no future presidential aspirant is likely to take a different
line—or to succeed if he does.[13]

After the General's reign France will still find herself with a powerful president and predominant executive. Because the prime minister
is responsible to Parliament and the system cannot work if he and
the President disagree, it may well be found necessary to bring the
parliamentary and presidential terms of office into line with one
another. But it will be hard for past habits to reassert themselves when
the government has control of parliamentary business; when the
President enjoys the prestige of direct election and wields the potent
weapons of referendum and dissolution; and while the electorate is
delighted with the new experience of stable government. The deputies
cannot return to their ancient sport of 'big-game hunting'—the inces-
sant harrying and frequent slaughter of governments—without breaking down strong constitutional, political and social barriers.

Many of the constitutional barriers represent the culmination of a
long development. Even under the Fourth Republic there was progress
towards a less disorderly method of arranging business, fewer interpellations, more government guidance during the passage of legislation,
a sharp reduction in the time spent on the budget, the abolition of the
private member's right to propose expenditure, a check on the veto
of the upper house, authority for the cabinet to decide the details
of legislation subject to principles laid down in Parliament, special
powers for the executive in emergency, and a usable right of dissolution. All these changes were already accepted by most sections of
political opinion (indeed some of the new solutions seem a good
deal less satisfactory than those proposed in the old regime). Thus
the constitutional barriers against any reversion to the past are more
than paper prohibitions.

The political barriers are still more formidable. Under de Gaulle,
repeated appeals to the people have given them opportunities which
are greatly appreciated to pronounce directly on their own future—
at referendums, in presidential campaigns, and in parliamentary elections which now turn on the choice of a government. Even if the

[13]The 1967 election showed the Gaullists capable of winning a (narrow)
victory on their own political appeal rather than on de Gaulle's prestige as a
national hero: see P. M. Williams and D. B. Goldey in *Parliamentary Affairs*
20.3 (Summer 1967).

political parties adapt themselves to the new regime and recover from the discredit into which most of them have fallen, they are unlikely ever to regain the monopoly of expressing the popular will which they cherished in the Third and Fourth Republics, and which led Paul Reynaud to tell the Assembly in 1962, 'Here and nowhere else is France'.[14] Perhaps de Gaulle went rather far in proclaiming on April 6 that year that the referendum was destined to play an ever-growing part in the nation's life, but he was right in claiming that it had entered too deeply into the political consciousness of the ordinary Frenchman to be eradicated easily. This change alone would blow a draught of fresh air through the corridors of the house without windows; and it gains added force from direct election of the chief executive, and from the slow evolution of the French party system.

Most decisive of all, the social basis for the old political order has been eroded rapidly in recent decades. In the past, a providential and intense conflict over the role of the Church in society served to determine political alignments and divert the voters from any inconvenient insistence on changing the social and economic system (with which most of them were in any case content). Independent political bosses competed and combined for control of a centralized and potentially oppressive State which was kept firmly subject to the collegial authority of the jealous parliamentarians. This style of politics reflected an individualist society in which the small-town notables—doctors, lawyers, teachers—organized rural opinion and exercised disproportionate political weight. That society was demographically and economically static, predominantly agricultural, largely self-sufficient, dominated by small farms and small firms, and politically responsive to the mystique of the peasant and the little man; it had very little State intervention in the economy (other than high tariffs) or effective mobilization of economic interests. But since those days French society has changed dramatically: population has risen, agriculture has declined, industry has spread, towns have grown fast, the means of communication have been transformed. Business pressure-groups, peasant organizations and workers' unions have developed into powerful social forces (by French if not by international standards), and strong political parties have come into being, first on the Left and later elsewhere. The European Common Market has done more than dismantle the old barriers to trade; it is both result and cause of the developments which are opening France more than ever before to influences as well as goods from the outside world.

These changes were under way well before 1958, but for a time they were accommodated by the old system. The old individualist groups continued to flourish, especially in 'backward France', and soon regained their lost power. For the democratic reformers, divided among themselves by the slowly dying clerical controversy, were too weak to meet alone the challenges of the new, dynamic but dangerous movements: Communism and Gaullism. They therefore enlisted the old parties as allies, at first subordinate but soon preponderant. Consequently, the Fourth Republic was a transitional period in which the free competition of political individuals and the *liberum veto* of strong parties and pressure-groups were both in operation together, hampering the executive and preventing difficult decisions being taken in time through the parliamentary machinery—especially in defence and colonial policy, where they could not be evaded for long. The failures created a mood of disillusion in which the parties opposed to the regime sometimes gathered alarming strength.

In 1958, therefore, public opinion accepted an institutional revolution which would have been strongly resisted a generation before, and, with experience of the new arrangements, began to develop a somewhat less anarchic attitude towards the citizen's relation with the State. In the new domestic and European setting, long-maturing social changes can at last find political expression. The old individualist parties and ideological conflicts seem hopelessly outmoded. Younger voters, including those of the Left, respond far less than their elders to historical memories and show far more interest in specific reforms. This new emphasis weakens those political organizations which are set in traditional ways and strengthens those which are most capable of adapting to a new situation. Up to 1967 the Gaullists had met the challenge far more effectively than others, had recruited more able and ambitious young newcomers, and had built themselves a reputation as a modernizing party. If their rivals are ever to compete they will have to follow suit. Moreover, the able and powerful corps of civil servants have come to appreciate the advantages of stable government for administrative responsibility and political foresight. Even though the Fourth Republic often allowed them to make policy by default, and even though many of them are highly critical of the Fifth, the old regime is as discredited among them as it is in the electorate generally. Therefore, as long as the parliamentarians cling to their hopes of a reaction, their chance of finding a useful if diminished role in the new system will meet resistance among both elite and mass opinion.

Developments in other countries reinforce these impressions. For the French case is only a spectacular instance of a general process. Throughout the democratic world, legislatures are losing power to the executive branch of government. Parliamentary scrutiny of expenditure through the annual budget is hard to reconcile with effective governmental control of the economy. Major reforms must be planned and carried out over long periods, and decisions to reorganize landholding or build a nuclear striking force commit the future far ahead.

When a powerful administrative service advises the politicians, the major pressure-groups will usually prefer to deal direct and early with the minister—or with his advisers—rather than challenge his decisions belatedly in Parliament. Sensible ministers try to make their proposals acceptable by consulting the interests affected from the beginning; the more they succeed in reaching a compromise to which everyone agrees, the less opportunity Parliament has to affect the result. Such developments are particularly evident in France, where a new executive in Brussels is now superimposed upon the ancient, powerful administration in Paris.

Writing at Parliament's lowest point in 1961, a leading political scientist of Gaullist sympathies compared its members to European countries which have lost their colonies. 'The course of events undermines the position of these displaced countries; they are aware of this and would be willing to adapt themselves to the change if they did not feel that their critics and detractors had gone from one extreme to the other. They do not regard themselves as deserving of blame and believe that they still have something of value to say and to teach, but they feel that their contribution is being spurned; they wish for a readjustment of the situation which, while marking the end of their hegemony, would leave their values intact.'[15] This readjustment has begun since he wrote, but rapid progress seems improbable at least in the short run. For the Gaullists have no motive of ideology or interest to undertake it, and while the traditional opposition leaders are themselves unlikely to get the chance, they may still keep the modernizing opposition from any early hope of power.

For a time, therefore, the Fifth Republic may survive in its present uneasy equilibrium. It is certainly no dictatorship, for Frenchmen enjoy freedom of speech and association and, having freely elected the Gaullists to power, still have regular opportunities to turn them out. It is not a government of separated powers like the United States, for France is a centralized country with no supreme court, where the Assembly is dominated by the cabinet and can be dissolved by the President. Yet neither is the government controlled, as in Britain, by the chosen leadership of the majority party. After de Gaulle the regime might evolve in the British direction, but even so it would remain something of an anomaly among the great democracies. For in that company France would still be the country in which the political executive, and the administrative technocracy behind it, have most autonomy in making decisions; and in which popular criticism, though not inaudible, finds expression least effectively through the nation's representative institutions. In the long run it will not be easy to reconcile this state of affairs with the historical traditions or current expectations of the French people.

[15]Léo Hamon in *International Social Science Journal* 13.4 (1961), p. 566.

LIST OF SOURCES

AMELLER, M. Les Questions instrument de contrôle parlementaire (Paris 1964).

ANON. A Constitution for the Fourth Republic (Washington, D.C., 1947).

AVRIL, P. Le Régime politique de la Vᵉ République (Paris 1964; 2nd ed. 1967);

AVRIL, P. "Le Vote bloqué": RDP 81.3 (June 1965), pp. 399-457.

BLUM, L. La Réforme gouvernementale (Paris 1919; 2nd ed., 1936).

BOUISSOU, M. "Le Statut de l'ORTF": RDP 80.6 (Nov. 1964), pp. 1109-97.

CAPITANT, R.: preface to Hamon, L., q.v.;

CAPITANT, R.: in Association française de Science politique, Les Institutions politiques de la France: Débat introduit par G. Vedel et F. Goguel (Paris 1964).

CHANDERNAGOR, A. Un Parlement, pour quoi faire? (Paris 1967).

CHAPSAL, J. La Vie politique en France depuis 1940 (Paris 1966).

CHARLOT, J. L'UNR: Etude du pouvoir au sein d'un parti politique (Paris 1967).

DEBRÉ, M. La Nouvelle Constitution (Paris 1958).

DELVOLVÉ, P. AND LESGUILLONS, H. Le Contrôle parlementaire sur la politique économique et budgétaire (Paris 1964).

DOGAN, M. in Association française de Science politique: Le Référendum de septembre et les Elections de novembre 1958 (Paris 1960);

DOGAN, M. in GOGUEL F., ed.: Le Référendum d'octobre et les Elections de novembre 1962 (Paris 1965).

DUSSAIFE, J. P. "Le Parlement face à la réforme des taxes sur le chiffre d'affaires": RFSP 16.3 (June 1966), pp. 521-31.

DUVERGER, M. Demain la République (Paris 1958).

GAULLE, C. DE: Mémoires de Guerre III: Le Salut (Paris 1959).

GOGUEL, F. "Bilan du travail législatif 1962-1966": Projet 13 (March 1967), pp. 283-99;

GOGUEL, F. "L'Evolution du pouvoir législatif en France"; unpublished paper read at Princeton, New Jersey, 16 April 1966.

GRANGE, J. see Guichard-Ayoub.

GUICHARD-AYOUB, E., et al: Etudes sur le Parlement de la Vᵉ République (Paris 1965).

HAMON, L. De Gaulle dans la République (Paris 1958);

HAMON, L. "Members of the French Parliament": International Social Science Journal 13.4 (1961), pp. 545-66;

HAMON, L. et al. "Vie et droit parlementaires": RDP 76.3 (May 1960), 79.6 (Nov. 1963), 80.1 (Jan. 1964), 82.2 (March 1967).

HARRISON, M. "The French experience of exceptional powers 1961": Journal of Politics 25.1 (Feb. 1963), pp. 139-58;

HARRISON, M. "Paris 5: Safe Seat": Political Studies 7.2 (June 1959), pp. 147-56.

HAYWARD, J. E. S. Private Interests and Public Policy: the experience of the French Economic and Social Council (London 1966).

LESGUILLONS, H. see Devolvé.

PRÉLOT, M. Pour comprendre la nouvelle constitution (Paris 1959).

PICKLES, D. The Fifth French Republic (2nd ed., London 1963).

RIMAREIX, G. AND TAVERNIER, Y. "L'élaboration et le vote de la loi complémentaire à la loi d'orientation agricole": RFSP 13.2 (June 1963), pp. 389-425.

ROIG, C. see Guichard-Ayoub.

TERRENOIRE, L. De Gaulle et l'Algérie (Paris 1964).

TRNKA, H. "Les Commissions mixtes paritaires": RDP 79.3 (May 1963), pp. 477-534.

WILLIAMS, P. M. Crisis and Compromise: Politics in the Fourth Republic (London 1964);

WILLIAMS, P. M. "The French referendum and election of October-November 1962": Parliamentary Affairs 16.2 (Spring 1963), pp. 165-73;

WILLIAMS, P. M. "The French Presidential election of 1965": ibid., 19.1 (Winter 1965-66), pp. 14-30;

WILLIAMS, P. M. AND D. B. GOLDEY: "The French general election of March 1967": ibid., 20.3 (Summer 1967);

WILLIAMS, P. M. AND M. HARRISON: De Gaulle's Republic (London 1960).

Sources not cited in the text for Parliament before 1958

BARTHELEMY, J. Essai sur le travail parlementaire et le système des commissions (Paris 1934).

BLAMONT, E. Les Techniques parlementaires (Paris 1958).

CAMPBELL, P. French Electoral Systems and Elections since 1789 (London, 2nd ed. 1965).

GOGUEL, F. Le Régime politique français (Paris 1955).

JOUVENEL, R. DE: La République des camarades (Paris, 1st ed. 1914).

LIDDERDALE, D. W. S. The Parliament of France (London 1951).

MIDDLETON, W. L. The French Political System (London 1932).

MUSELIER, F. Regards neufs sur le Parlement (Paris 1956).

SHARP, W. R. The Government of the French Republic (New York 1939).

SIEGFRIED, A. Tableau des partis en France (Paris 1930); trans. as France, a study in nationality (New Haven 1930).

WILLIAMS, P. M., HARRISON, M. et al., "France 1958" in Butler, D. E., ed., Elections Abroad (London 1959).